What We Wore

What We Wore

An Offbeat Social History
of Women's Clothing,
1950 to 1980

ELLEN MELINKOFF

Quill, New York 1984

Library of Congress Cataloging in Publication Data

Melinkoff, Ellen.
    What we wore.

    1. Costume—United States—History—20th century.
2. Fashion—United States—History—20th century.
I. Title.
[GT615.M44   1984]   391'.2'0904   83-17725
ISBN 0-688-02839-X
ISBN 0-688-02228-6 (pbk.)

Printed in the United States of America

First Quill Edition

1   2   3   4   5   6   7   8   9   10

BOOK DESIGN BY JAMES UDELL

To Marc

Acknowledgments

I would like to express my appreciation to the women who responded to my letter asking them to tell me what they wore:
Sherry Alberoni, Pamela J. Baergen, Karen Berman, Tristine Berry, Joan Borgman, Helen Gurley Brown, Michele Burgess, Peggy Byrnes, Sandy Calin, Gloria Casvin, Manuela Cerruti, Sara B. Chase, Linda Dahl, Barbara Diamond, Anita Engel, Nora Ephron, Linda Finch, Eileen Fond, Helen Foster, Anna Lee Fuchs, Laurie Burrows Grad, Sally Henderson, Ginger Hill, Rose Mary Kimble, Nancy Kinney, Judy Lamm, Kelly Lange, Caroline Latham, Gloria List, Pat Mathis, Lyn Messner, M. Miller, Janice Morgan, Regina Neuman, Rae Neumen, Marilyn Overholt, Beth Padon, Joan Padon, Nancie L. Porter, Rochelle Reed, Christine Robinson, Emby Searson, Alice Short, Shelley Stephens, Susan Stern, Dawn Sturgill, Annette Swanberg, Ailene Watson, Anne Wehrer, Sandy Whitehurst, Caroline Winslow, Joanna Wood, Pansy Yee, Carolyn Zucker.

I also appreciate the help I received from: Cole of California, Diane Von Furstenberg Creative Services, the Fashion Institute of Technology in Los Angeles, Glen-Raven Mills, Jantzen, CPC Corporation, and Vanity Fair. Special thanks to Sears Roebuck Archives for making their catalog pictures available to me, and to Nancy Kinney at Western Costume Company's Research Library for graciously permitting me to use her library's facilities.

Contents

What We Wore

In the past thirty years, we have dressed in the hoops of a Spanish infanta, the beads of the gypsies, the bell bottoms from the crew of the H.M.S. *Pinafore,* the caftans of Moroccan tribal chieftains, the fishnet tights and short skirts of Forty-second Street hookers, the cummerbunds and ruffled shirts of matadors, the chemises of flappers, the three-piece pinstriped suits of Wall Street brokers—all in the name of fashion. We have gone from covering all, to exposing all, to selective exposure. We exchanged the slavish conformity of the fifties for the slavish nonconformity of the hippie years till we found the sense of individuality that we enjoy today.

What we wore and what we liked were not always the same thing. We never really liked girdles or garter belts, dressmaker bathing suits, sacks, muumuus, seamed stockings, or hot pants. Some garments we wore because convention dictated and technology limited. When we did like a style, it was often because we were set up to do so by the fashion industry, by television, by fashion magazines, by mothers, by men, by best friends, by the overwhelming examples set by the most popular girls.

The most immediate influence was peer pressure. To sport a Villager shirtwaist, Capezio flats, or perfectly faded jeans when the occasion called for a Villager shirtwaist, Capezio flats, or perfectly faded jeans put the wearer in the catbird seat. It gave one a certain amount of control and an almost endless self-confidence. In 1967 to be the only girl on the block *not* wearing a mini was tantamount to social leprosy. To wear the same mini in 1977 was social leprosy again.

To stay in fashion is to go with the flow. If we women are the pragmatists that we are so often touted to be, it affects our dress too. Once a new style is on a roll, we know it's best not to be too firmly attached to the old look. And while we have been able to call a halt to, or at least redirect, a few fashions, we know that we are not in total control. At best, we have only a veto power, which we exercised with the sack and the midi. We are able to nix a new style and stick with what we have been wearing, but for the most part, we cannot create a new one. Lace tights, stretch pants, bikinis, pea jackets—like everything else we have worn—were offered for our consideration. Years ago, we didn't realize we could say, "No, thank you." Designers became accustomed to having unquestioned authority, and when we finally refused to wear one of their dictates, the sack, they were stunned.

Despite our newfound tongues, we still wait for the new looks to be announced each year: the cut of jeans, the width of lapels, the newest shades, Some of us have been playing this fashion game for thirty years or more, and we still go with the flow.

How does it feel to look back three decades, to remember, to examine what we wore? Can we go home again? Can we look at old pictures of ourselves in minis, hot pants, hoopskirts, and tulle prom dresses without flinching?

To find out what we remember about what we wore, I wrote to women all over the country asking them to think back on their long-lost, long-forgotten clothes. The responses came from all over, from women who live and lived very different life-styles: teachers, social workers, cooks, housewives, an ex-Mouseketeer, a TV anchor, writers, editors, an interior designer, librarians, business-women, lawyers.

Some were wearing New Look suits in the early fifties, some, Dale Evans cowgirl outfits. Whether they were five or twenty-five, women still remembered their best outfits from those days, and all their best ones since. The tenor of so many responses was twofold:

"How could I have worn this?" followed by "But I remember how good I felt in it." Each woman who responded could have filled a book by herself. Once the women sat down to write, all the silly fads and fashions (like buck bags and sword pins and Jamaica shorts) leaped to mind. Ensembles, and the occasions they were worn, were recalled in detail.

The letters I received varied in length from one paragraph to six single-spaced typed pages. There were common themes (what ankle bracelets meant, how pointy shoes hurt, the troubles with hoops) and individual eccentricities. Some universal truths showed up:

First of all, we have put up with an amazing amount of discomfort. In the name of conformity, or of finding a man, it seems we would wear anything: girdles, spike heels, skirts that barely covered our butts.

I was also amazed at how much the letters echoed the actual history of fashion I was researching in the library. The woman who said she was so turned off by the midi that she turned to pants was speaking for most of her generation.

Junior high school, even more than high school, seemed to be the period of strongest conformity. It was crucial to wear the right socks, shoes, purse, belt, and skirt. It really did make the difference between popularity and wallflowerhood. Those were the rules we played by, and though junior high girls in the fifties and sixties would never have used this term, we played hardball. To have sweater sets in six shades could set you up for life (especially if you never left your hometown). We all had "rich girls" in our schools—the ones with the angora sweaters, camel's hair coats, fox collars, and assorted other animalia that set apart the haves and the have-nots. We envied them, studied them, and when we could, we copied them.

Every girl seemed to be copying, conforming to the other girls in school. No one said she was the trendsetter that all eyes were on.

In the fifties, we spent less money on clothes than we do today. We put more stock in serviceable everyday wear; being neat and clean was show enough. Special occasions were marked with new

dresses, new hats, and new shoes. Today, every outfit must be fashionable, eye-catching, accessorized to the hilt. For school, for work,
for play, we dress with the attention and money we once saved for
proms. We don't dress so fancy anymore, but we don't dress "serviceable" either.

Dress up is something we do a couple of times a year. There
was a time when high heels, stockings, gloves, and fussy dresses
were typical date clothes. They've been replaced by silk shirts and
designer jeans or upscale jogging suits. It's a whole new mind-set.
Our mothers, more deeply ingrained in the old ways, have a hard
time seeing that we are dressed up enough for most of the occasions
in our lives. They fret that we should be wearing a wool dress or
suit to Thanksgiving dinner, or a gingham sundress and white high
heels to the Fourth of July picnic.

We have lived through the most outlandish stages in acceptabil-
ity of office wear. After minis and thigh-high boots, tie-dye tops and
faded overalls, granny dresses and hiking boots, we have settled into
a conservative way of dressing compared with the peculiarities of a
decade ago.

There are always some women who get so fixated on the aesthetic of their early years that they are unable to adapt to changes as
their lives progress. In the fifties, I used to look at what I called
"the pompadour ladies"—middle-aged women who looked like they
were still living in 1942. *Haute* Andrews Sisters. To my eyes, they
appeared pitifully dated compared with their contemporaries, who
were wearing shirtwaists, softer hairdos, and much less rouge.
Today, I see *my* contemporaries in their late thirties, still caught up
in the Jackie-Kennedy–early-sixties look. They are unable to appear
in public without eyeliner or teased hair. I see others who look like
aging hippies, refusing to trade their wire-rimmed granny glasses
for newer designer frames. They are the pompadour ladies of our
generation. Some are unable to see that eyebrows are softer, lips,
redder, and that no one wears hip-hugger bell bottoms or platform
shoes anymore. I think women who marry and settle down early
tend to retain the style of their courtship years. Women who remain out in the world longer have to adapt to survive. We have had

moments of mini-ness, hippie-ness, Annie Hall-ness. Today we are trying to come to grips with punk and Norma Kamali—trying to adapt without looking like we're pandering to pubescent tastes.

To discover the story behind the clothes, the why of we wore what we did, I pored over thirty years of *Vogue, Mademoiselle, Time, Newsweek, Look,* the Sears catalog, and every issue of *Life.* The fashion magazines showed what was being sold. *Life,* in its real-people stories, showed what was being worn, and documented fads and fashions with almost equal weight. It reported on Paris styles as well as teen crazes like sewing rickrack on sweatshirts. *Life* captured socialites, suburban housewives, office workers, college girls, subdebs, and celebrities. It not only documented, it advised: It gave suggestions on how to starch crinolines, on the correct length of the sack, and what to do about static electricity in Orlon.

I would spend an afternoon in the library studying pedal pushers, minis, crop tops, spaghetti straps, then walk out onto the street to see real women wearing much of what I'd been studying: She's fifties. She's sixties. She's seventies. Some were studied re-creations of period dressing, a typical Los Angeles phenomenon. Others were merely pompadour ladies, blissfully unaware that someone was seeing them as a period piece (besides, their husbands probably loved them that way). But most were probably oblivious to their period look. It wasn't a slavish re-creation of times gone by, just a key item like a pants style, shoes, or a skirt length. There were minis on girls who weren't even born when Mary Quant opened her boutique in Chelsea. Black flats. Peasant blouses and flounced skirts on women who thought of it as the latest look rather than one of the oldest.

I was surprised at how many of the clothes of the past thirty years I still liked, could imagine wearing, and wished were still for sale. Many items looked as if they could be worn today, with a little updating, not as a period look, not as thrift-shop finds, but as clothes that could be found now in fashion magazines and stores. Canvas espadrilles, bulky sweaters, pedal pushers, polo coats, blazers, plaid skirts come to mind. (Always casual clothes, though. Dressy styles now look camp. They were higher style to begin with—more in and suddenly more out. Casual clothes were meant to last a few seasons.) The underwear, the makeup, and the hairdos remain dated. But the clothes are surprisingly adaptable. Why was I in such a hurry to throw everything out at the first hint of *démodé?*

Women's styles seem to be a cyclical reiteration of the same few modes: Ivy League, ethnic, mini-mod, conservative, and romantic. Many of us found a favorite style twenty or thirty years ago and have kept it our favorite ever since. It may change names (Ivy League has become preppie), but the basic look is the same. We change sides as infrequently as we change political parties. It was hard to stay true to Ivy League aesthetics in a mini-mod year, and some accommodation was necessary (shortening shirtwaists and wearing a few tailored minis), but the inner Ivy League feeling remained and bided its time until the style rode high again. Most of us are too fashion conscious not to go with the flow in some measure. Few of us refuse to dabble at least in a new style. But all of us—Ivy Leaguers, peasant-ethnics, Edwardian-romantics, tailored-conservatives—have to sit out a few rounds. Those are the years we don't spend as much on clothes, buying just the bare minimum to appear somewhat in tune. We think we have had a change of heart about clothes, that they are not so important to us anymore, but it's just that there isn't much in the stores that appeals to us. The next year we are back to our old clotheshorse tricks.

These days it's almost as if nobody has to do much sitting out. Everything seems to be in at the same time. When we look at other women, we aren't quite sure if they're wearing something brand-new or something from two years ago. It's a heady experience and we should all take advantage of it. Who knows how long this live-and-let-live attitude will prevail.

It's hard to classify today's clothes. Perhaps in ten years we'll be able to sum up the dress of the eighties. Now it's so much easier (and really much more fun) to look back at the fifties.

The Fifties

The year 1950 was not a turning point in American fashion. What we were wearing then had become fashionable a few years before true midcentury. A quick look at forties fashions will be our jumping-off point.

The war-years aesthetic was severe and economical—short skirts and man-tailored jackets. During the war, women not only did men's jobs but came perilously close to wearing men's clothing. Comfort before femininity. Besides, the men were at the front. Who needed ruffles? While few women actually wore trousers, most took to the tailored styles of the time.

After the war, women were encouraged to give their wrenches back to the returning GIs and go back home to raise the baby-boom generation. To foster that *Kinder, Kirche, Küche* role, women's fashions became softer, more feminine. If we were to act like women, we had to dress like women. If we were to act like wives and mothers, we had to dress like wives and mothers.

In 1947, French couturier Christian Dior introduced the New Look with its decidedly female silhouette. The style was the antithesis of the austere war-years look. Natural shoulders replaced the heavy padded ones of the early forties. Mannish notched collars and lapels were supplanted by flat, neck-hugging collars. Waists were tightly fitted and skirts were long. The New Look was extremely fitted, and extremely womanly. Breasts were pushed up and spot-lighted, waists were pared down to an anatomical minimum, and hips were curved. Woman as hourglass.

The style was epitomized (*epitome* was a big word in the fifties, especially with intellectually pretentious high schoolers) by the New Look suit: a tightly fitted jacket (totally hiding the blouse, if there was room for one underneath) that flared over the hips, topping a straight or gored skirt. Sleeves were long and fitted. To pull off this look successfully required a considerable amount of infrastructure, the Sherman tank line of corsetry. The natural female figure was merely raw material that had to be poured, molded, whittled to per-fection. How did it feel to be living sculpture? Awful. But we en-dured in the name of womanhood. This idealized feminine attitude lasted through most of the fifties, accommodating new designs but holding fast to its part in the sexually dimorphic scheme of the decade.

Fifties fashions reflected the shifting life-styles of the postwar years. Families moved to the suburbs and bought their first televi-sion. Women stayed home and raised the kids. When those kids became teenagers, they danced a lot. *That* was the fifties. In terms of clothes, the life-style meant feminine looks, "at-home" wear, car coats, big business for subdeb and teen clothing manufacturers.

Of course, we never thought, "Ah ha, we've moved to Levit-town. Now we'll need car coats." But when we moved to Levit-town, the car coats were in the stores waiting for us. When we turned into style-conscious twelve-year-olds, subdeb departments sprang up to clothe us. Designers seemed to anticipate (or was it create?) our every need.

But suburbia and subdebs were minor influences compared with television. TV opened up the world to us, including the fashion world. It let us see "what people were wearing" with an intensity, an immediacy we had never had. Before that time we relied on *Life*, fashion magazines, and movies for guidance. But those media were remote and told us what a model or movie star had worn months ago. With TV, we could see what Dorothy Kilgallen was wearing tonight, what Bess Myerson had on this afternoon, and what Justine and Pat on *American Bandstand* had worn to their high school this very day. To see it was to want it. We saw more, we wanted more, we spent more. The golden age of consumerism had begun. We wanted newer, faster. Styles, if only how to roll our socks or tie a scarf, reached us quicker. So did the next styles, precipitating both new hat and old hat.

Television shaped a new level of fashion consciousness even in what we wore to watch it. People stayed home and invited friends, especially those without TVs, to watch with them. That called for a new fashion posture—literally. Floor-length plaid skirts or velveteen pants were far more graceful for an artful sprawl in front of the set than regular clothes. In fact, the whole concept of at-home clothes arrived with television. The better to watch Lucy or Uncle Miltie or Sid and Imogene in, my dear. *Life* magazine's layout on the new at-home styles called them "semi-public pyjamas," a much more unwieldy term than "at-home," which prevailed. Stay-at-home slippers came into vogue, perfect for wearing into the kitchen to pick up a tray of canapes during a commercial. Velvety mules, satiny sandals, and pancake-soled, foldable flats came in little bags. Suddenly shoes that were never meant to be worn out-of-doors became practical.

Kids in the fifties, the first television generation, had one favorite outfit, cowboy suits. The TV cowboys and girls, Roy and Dale and Gene most of all, were our "haute cowture." Parents encouraged the style, bought it. It was cute, harmless, and very American, but nevertheless it was a television-heightened fashion. From the day the TV set was brought home, we wanted to emulate our television heroes, and not strictly for Halloween. We put on our fringed vests, holsters, and hats to strut around the living room and the backyard every chance we could. We *were* Dale and Roy, nobody could tell us differently. We never tired of the charade. We had our pictures taken with our prized outfits on (the pictures became the prizes long after the costumes were thrown away).

Roy Rogers, of course, was *the* cowboy. We might remember his clean-cut good looks and chalk up his popularity to that. But he was a businessman-cowboy. In 1953, *Life* featured a four-page ad-

For little girls in the fifties, a Dale Evans outfit topped Christmas wish lists: fancy yokes and fringes, guns with holsters, and (if they were lucky) boots too. It was twenty-five years between Dale Evans cowgirl getups and Ralph Lauren's prairie clothes. We've come a long way, baby! (Sears, Roebuck and Company)

vertisement (and those were big pages) of Roy Rogers items for sale, not just vests and toy guns and hats, but lunch boxes, bedspreads, picture frames, clocks, socks, pajamas, gloves, and TV chairs. Everything had Roy or Dale or Trigger emblazoned on the side. It was just as slick and all-pervasive an advertising-merchandising package as the eighties *Star Wars* or *E.T.* glut.

The cowboy style was strictly a grammar school phenomenon. As we became increasingly sophisticated, or so we thought, we cast aside our fringed vests for crinolines and cinch belts.

The extremely full-skirted, crinoline-cum-hoop look was only one of the fifties silhouettes, but the absurdity, the upkeep, and the sheer tension of wearing those skirts have kept the memories so alive that we remember the fifties for its petticoats alone.

Looking back at our full skirts, it's difficult to believe that we were actually in high fashion at the time. It wasn't just another kids-only thrill like the Dale Evans outfits. We would like to think that full skirts must have been some aberrant style, something only junior high school girls (always particularly adept at aberrant styles) would take a fancy to. What could such girls, with four-feet-in-diameter hoops under pastel broadcloth skirts set off with saddle shoes and ankle socks, have to do with high fashion? We saw the style on TV, or on another girl who had seen it on television. We wanted it. We wore it. Peer pressure was the only force we knew. We copied each other, augmenting as we did. Five crinolines were better than four. Five and a hoop were better than five without a hoop. In no time, the skirt was as extreme as the one worn by the Spanish infanta. We never, ever stopped to wonder where such a fad originated.

But this was long before street fashions and idiosyncratic dressing were in vogue. So somebody "in charge" had had to set the fad in motion.

It was Ann Fogarty. The petite New York designer was her own best advertisement, posing for pictures in dresses held out to there with at least two stiff-as-boards petticoats. It was a Seventh Avenue fashion after all, called in the fashion world the Paper Doll Look. Ann Fogarty's silhouette, unknown to us copycats in algebra class, was our ideal.

This Paper Doll Look wasn't nearly as simple to achieve as its name implied. Traditional cotton and lace petticoats wouldn't do. Netting would. Horsehair was even better, better meaning stiffer but never meaning more comfortable. These petticoats itched, but they did the job. The goal was to get as few slips as possible to stick out as far as possible. *Life* advised us to restarch crinolines and press while damp. "Better still," the magazine suggested, "use shellac over a blotter."

Soon, no amount of netting, starch, or shellac would make the slips stand out far enough to suit us. The hoop seemed like a much better solution. It wouldn't pack down like crinolines did. It didn't need as much attention—you just removed the hoop before washing the slip and threaded it back on a clean one. But what the hoop offered in easy care, it took away in sheer unmanageability. To maneuver aisles, staircases, and wind gusts required an incredible amount of dexterity, practically an advanced degree in physics. To flip up the hoop was instant mortification (mortification being always very close to the surface for a teenager).

The hoop could not be worn by itself, like a hula hoop suspended under the skirt. It had to be softened, the ridge disguised. The perfect hoop stood just about two inches shorter than the skirt hem, with a finishing layer of crinoline on top. The hoop line was not supposed to show. VHL (visible hoop line), as we could have called it, was anathema. Never a bend in the downward slide of the skirt. The line from waist to hem had to be a perfectly straight line, 45 degrees from the floor. The ultimate compliment to a hoop wearer was to wonder, "Is she wearing a hoop?" The hoop had to flow and float like the Champagne Lady's petticoats. To attain such a profile, we were willing to sacrifice more than a little comfort. We allowed our legs to be scratched like fashion-crazed junior *penitentes.* We let below-freezing winter drafts whirl up our legs. We knew we would be admired for what we were wearing.

Full skirts had to be at least four or five (and often more) yards in circumference to drape properly over the hoop and its crinolines. That's a lot of fabric to draw up into a smaller-the-better-and-twenty-inches-wouldn't-be-too-small waistline. The gathers were

Sandra Dee may have received bad news here, judging from the way she's emoting, but she should have taken comfort in knowing that she had the ideal fifties figure—milkmaid breasts, twenty-inch waist, and who knows whether there were hips under all those crinolines. (Universal Pictures Company)

tolerable in light cotton broadcloth skirts, plain or plaid, which is
what most of us wore. But the high-fashion skirts were done in
wool. Five yards of wool is a weighty proposition. They compacted
the five petticoats into looking like two or three. A hoop looked
more oval than round as it tried to accommodate the imbalance of
seams and plackets. If hoops were silly with cotton skirts, they were
asinine with wool ones. We literally had lost all sense of proportion,
stopping just short of bringing back the farthingale.

Full skirts, in our fifties mind-set, had two advantages: They
totally obscured less-than-perfect hips and they emphasized a small
waist. Wasp waist, we called it. Full skirts made a not-so-small waist
small. And by adding a three-inch-wide cinch belt, voila! Scarlett
redux. Wide belts were an important fashion accessory—elastic
cinches, leather, or plastic (new and exciting and nothing-cheap-
about-it plastic). The wider, the better; the tighter, the better. Belts
with grommets always showed pull lines, and plastic belts with
unreinforced holes stretched into most unattractive tears. Elastic
cinches were the best because they hooked closed, neatly and effi-
ciently, and helped keep blouses from slipping up.

Circle skirts were an effective way to cut down the bulk of full
skirts. The hemlines could be more than adequately full while the
waist was a mere twenty to twenty-two inches. Wool skirts were
lightened considerably, made tolerable. A circle skirt still took a lot
of fabric, but everything took a lot of fabric back then. We couldn't
imagine a skirt taking less than a yard as it would in miniskirt days.

Felt was the fabric of choice for circle skirts. Felt was newly
available in fashionable colors like pink, lavender, and turquoise,
and became a practical solution to an impractical fad. It was more
adept at covering hoop ridges, and the hemline could just be cut to
the right length. Getting an even hem on most fabrics could take
hours. Besides, we could just glue on such cute appliqués: guitars,
"See You Later Alligator," and, of course, poodles.

If ever an animal was associated with the look of a decade, it
was the poodle and the fifties. As early as 1951, *Life* magazine
showed a model sporting a felt skirt with a poodle appliquéd on the
side. The model, wearing just a tube top for a blouse, held the leash
of a real, live poodle. (It was a black-and-white photo, but surely the

skirt was pink and the poodle black.) Poodle skirts remain a clichéd memory of fifties fashion.

By the next year, women had cut their pageboys and ponytails into poodle clips. These short, curly hairdos were almost as revolutionary as bobs had been in the twenties. They looked crisp and free, but required considerable upkeep. To look perfect, the poodle clip had to be cut every two weeks. To keep it curly required a permanent, probably a Toni or a Lift, or up to 125 pin curls at night. And while the cut looked daring and stylish, it wasn't very becoming to most women. The curls were too short, too tight to compliment any but the prettiest heads. A head of curls should have a softening effect, but poodle clips could look quite harsh.

In 1953, Italian cuts made the poodle clip look dated. The difference between the two styles was only an inch or so in most places, but that extra length turned a difficult style into a flattering one. An Italian cut was shaggier than the poodle (more like an unpampered poodle). Shaggy but sculptured, it was described. Sexy spit curls curved over the cheeks. The Italian cut was easy to maintain (fewer hairnets, fewer perms), and it didn't take a Gina Lollobrigida to carry it off.

The fifties were a time of solid, Kansas-in-August Americana, but we were fascinated with foreign influences on our lives and clothes. It didn't take much to make us feel exotic. The French were viewed with suspicion. Their designers were always foisting new, too chic, too outlandish designs on us. We waited each year for the announcement from Paris regarding next year's hemline. Newspapers and magazines played along, giving front-page coverage to the long-anticipated, dreaded measurement. (Strangely, hemlines were given in inches from the floor, fourteen, sixteen, or twenty inches, regardless of the fact that leg lengths and shoe styles varied.) The newsworthiness of this event heightened our impression that we were powerless to rebel. Paris would tell us what was fashionable. When the word finally leaked out, the top couturiers specifying an inch shorter or three inches longer, it was given the authority of a papal bull. We meekly made adjustments to our skirts so we wouldn't look provincial.

Only Paris was seen as an adversary in fashion. Other places

"Summer party dress, worn by pert young Debbie Reynolds . . ." the copy for this fifties press release began. It went on to describe the neckline, with those silly button tabs all around, as "youthful." But the dropped waist and long hemline make it look like Debbie pulled this one out of her mother's closet. The shoes too. (Warner Brothers)

were viewed as spots from which to draw creative inspiration. Spanish toreadors, Italian gondoliers, Mexican peasants—New York designers adapted these native costumes, and we adored them. They made us feel worldly, exotic, but never ethnic. Who knew about ethnic in the fifties? We just wanted, and got, a touch of the world-out-there.

We wanted to sashay around Levittown in white ruffled blouses and tight black pants. The cummerbund was an essential part of this matador mania. We wore it first as part of the total toreador outfit (bolero, shirt, pants, and, if we were really snappy, a bicorne hat), and then began to accessorize dresses and skirts with it. We did get

The extras in this still from Tammy and the Bachelor *are a study in the major styles of the fifties. The blonde at the extreme left wears an always-a-safe-choice black top with a checkered circle skirt. The woman in front of her, sporting an Italian haircut, wears pedal pushers and a man-tailored shirt out-side her pants. This casual outfit came perilously close to being sloppy by fifties standards. Good thing the shirt is freshly pressed. The gingham-dressed inge-nue wears a hoopskirt to keep her skirt the requisite three feet in diameter and emphasizes her waist with a wide white belt. One of the women leaning out the window wears an Italian stripe knit top.* (Universal Pictures Company)

a little bored with cinch belts, day after day. The cummerbund stayed around for many years, and none of us seemed to notice that the word was not pronounced "cumberbund."

Black pants were a stock item in most fifties and sixties wardrobes. They weren't limited to matador costumes. With a striped T-shirt, they looked Italian and even took an Italian name, capris. The name stuck and continues to haunt us. Even today, forty-year-olds have to fight *not* to call all pants "capris." The stripes on those knit tops were called Italian or Roman stripes.

In the early fifties, the Santa Fe look was having its first go-round. *Life* featured squaw skirts and Navajo blouses as summer wear. Rickrack-trimmed, bright cotton broomstick skirts with three gathered tiers were brought back east from vacations to the Southwest. Jennifer Jones's half-breed *Duel in the Sun* character was perfectly dressed for suburban patio parties. Authentic Mexican huaraches were a touch too ethnic for us then (they needed the stamp of approval of the antithesis-of-ethnic surfers to become popular in later years), but canvas espadrilles were an acceptable substitute.

While we didn't really want to know about it (preferring to think it was strictly a matter of hemlines), French designers did have considerable influence over what we wore. The New Look proved this fact but that was far from an isolated instance of Parisian power. The Spanish-born but Paris-working designer Balenciaga, with his high-priced couture, seemed far removed from the baby-boom mothers in the American suburbs. Most of us had never heard of him or remembered his name until years later, if then. But Balenciaga's 1954 look had almost as much impact on fashion everywhere as Dior's New Look had had seven years earlier. And again, it filtered down to us, in Peoria, in Plainsville, in Poughkeepsie.

Balenciaga broke with the extremely fitted style of the time and created a semifitted look. The New Look had called for a narrow waistline, flattering only to those who were thin and stayed that way. An extra ten pounds required expensive or time-consuming alterations. Balenciaga did make life a little bit easier for us.

Once again, suits defined the look at its ideal. Jackets were still darted in front, but in a figure-skimming rather than figure-hugging way. The jacket back was straight, bordering on boxy. Instead of a dainty neck-hugging collar, Balenciaga's new collar stood away from the neck. Shoulder seams were dropped a bit and sleeves were shortened from wrist length to below the elbow. Skirts were straight. It was just a small segue from the form-fitting New Look, but it was a crucial move. Not only did this look affect style on every level, but it opened the door for the unfitted designs of the future, the overblouses, chemises, trapezes—which were spectacularly innovative.

Dior suit or Balenciaga outfit, gloves were required to finish off the look. Flip through the pages of fifties fashion magazines, and you'll find that almost every model is wearing gloves. No suits were ever shown without them, and very few dresses. Women in those years had drawers filled with gloves: long, short, white, off-white, black—but mainly white. We can explain away the modesty, the rigid corsetry, the high necklines, but what was this obsession for gloving our hands in near-surgical splendor? Imagine wearing gloves today for anything but warmth. Yet in the fifties, glove manufacturers were major advertisers in fashion magazines. Shortie, opera length, gauntlet—each occasion, each ensemble had only one possible, one correct glove style. We were so afraid of appearing in public "improperly" dressed that our only thought was to wear the proper gloves, never whether to wear them at all.

When nylon gloves appeared in 1951, they were ballyhooed as "perfect from early spring till late summer." We bought them, of course. Better than cotton, they dried in an hour. But nylon gloves made our palms even sweatier. The sweat could dry in less than an hour too.

The colors we wore had a rigid set of rules also. Once we were told what colors went with each other, we stuck with those concepts. Mother handed the palette down to daughter. Our clothes were not artists' canvases. We were not artists. We were technicians.

Black and white were the cornerstones of every woman's wardrobe. Every outfit had one or the other as its basic color—neutral,

we called it then. Whether we chose black or white depended solely
on the time of year. Black was worn between Labor Day and Memorial Day; white from Memorial Day to Labor Day. So what if
there was a heat spell in early October or a cold snap in early June.
Rules were rules. Beige shoes could be worn when black was just
too offensive to our sensibilities, when it was 90 degrees and Labor
Day two weeks behind us. And black patent, but *never* plain black
leather, was acceptable in the summer. It sounds more like a Jane
Austen novel than something we did just thirty years ago.

Black was *the* basic color: black shoes, black purses, black belts.
We thought everything "went with" black. How could we have
ever thought of such a strong color as being neutral? We liked black
with mint green, with lavender, with turquoise. It never struck us as
too heavy, too strong, or too unbalanced.

We always wore black shoes, ranging from plain flats and T-
straps to suede pumps and sandals for evening. Capezio had it all
over other flats. They knew just how to cut them, low and sexy.
Flat as a pancake. The curve of the top was cut low, with just
enough leather to keep the shoes on, revealing a provocative hint of
toe cleavage. We had never heard of "less is more," but we lived it
in our Capezios. Cheaper imitations never pulled it off.

Even though we couldn't wait to shuck our grammar school
Mary Janes (straps meant you were too much of a baby to know
how to keep your shoes on without them), a few years later we had
to have T-straps. T-straps and double T-straps were so in that we
forgot all about our rush to dump our Mary Janes.

Once we got our black accessories going, and if there was some
money left over, we could consider navy or brown shoes. But that
would require matching navy or brown purses and belts, and practically a whole new wardrobe. (And they would have to be the exact
same shade of navy or dark brown as the shoes.) The black-based
closet was filled wth black skirts, black capris, and little black
dresses. You couldn't possibly wear navy shoes with a black skirt.

Black was considered safe and expected when it was the color of
skirts and capris; it was thought daring for tights and turtlenecks,
topped with a tweedy jumper or skirt. So intellectual, so avant-

garde. No matter how many outfits like that we saw, we thought every one of them reflected a personal creativity on the part of the wearer.

Black on the bottom was for everyday wear as well as for dress-up. Black on top was for beatniks or formal occasions. The black top, in any style from strapless tube to halter to V-neck, and a full skirt became a nighttime uniform. One step away from the little black dress. Black top and white lace skirt—wow!

Black dresses were every woman's answer to the problem of what to wear. Every time there was any indecision, out came the black dress. If there were ten women at a party, nine would be in black. We maintained our individuality with a neckline variation or a bright scarf. But it was a futile attempt. The black always dominated.

Black was our crutch. Could we have ever imagined a time when we wouldn't have a pair of black shoes, when camel would take over as the dominant, yet neutral, shoe and purse color? Or that it would be possible to live without a black dress in the closet for any and all emergencies? We felt safe with black. It symbolized sexiness and adulthood. Black on young girls was frowned upon. Our mothers told us we would look like old crones in it and forced us into namby-pamby pastels. *They* (and we also) knew black had power behind it. A first black dress was a significant event, a coming out, and no mere girl could pull off such a severe color.

White was our summer standby. In winter it was strictly for collars, cuffs, gloves, underwear, and blouses. Perhaps a few women wore "winter-white" wools but these were really cream colored. White blouses were year-rounders. Every woman had several. We bought practically the same Peter Pan or Ivy League style over and over again. And we ironed them over and over again.

White shorts, pedal pushers, and capris were summer staples and best worn with white flats. Flats were polished several times a week and could sport a whole bottle of Shinola by the end of August. White permanent-pleated skirts, in new washable synthetics, turned up in the stores in time for summer 1958. Another uniform. We were amassing wardrobes of uniforms. White duck pants were not so easy care, but that didn't stop us. By 1959, we felt luxurious in white fake-fur coats. They were okay in winter.

Black and white were so basic they were taken for granted. Pink was an exciting discovery. If the poodle was the animal of the fifties, pink was the color of the decade. It was exhilarating to wear. Even the palest, softest baby pink was daring, worldly. Diana Vreeland called it "the navy blue of India," meaning it was worn as a neutral there, but we couldn't imagine comparing a *real* neutral like navy with such a frivolous color.

We never explored pink. We wore it with black or gray. That, we were sure, was its destiny. We were warned that pink clashed with red and orange and could *never* be worn with those colors. Only clowns would do that. We wanted to appear fashionable, not trendy. Pair a pink oxford-cloth shirt with gray flannel Bermudas or a skirt (with perhaps an Ivy League buckle in the back of the waist)—that was style. Or how about a pink brocade party dress to stand out in a room filled with conforming crows, all in black. The height of daring: pink gloves.

Our infatuation with pink didn't end with clothes. Washers and dryers were pink. In 1955, magazine ads for the Dodge Lancer showed the most daring color combination: "heather rose, jewel black, and sapphire white." Now there was a car. In 1956, we bought pink irons and dinner plates and electric frypans. Then pink vacuum cleaners. Then pink Naugahyde cushions wrapped around black wrought-iron chair bases. We wore pink. We decorated pink. We drove pink.

We were intrigued with other pastels—aqua, lavender, mint green—but they never captivated us like pink did. But whatever the hue, we applied the same rules: lavender with black, or aqua with black.

Some women understood the power of black (and the impotence of mint green) more clearly than the rest of us. Audrey Hepburn did.

While we looked askance at French designers, we embraced, adored, revered the French designers' dream girl, Audrey Hepburn. She was our dream too. We didn't want her to model our

When we first discovered Audrey Hepburn, she was pure gamin. She made the term "waif" a high compliment. She could take a black pullover sweater, calico print jumper (jumpers were new in those days), and Capezio pancake flats and make those more appealing than anything Paris could turn out. No matter what our size or shape, in our heart of hearts we were gamins too. (Larry Edmunds)

Half gamin, half woman of the world at this point, Audrey Hepburn in her black outfit makes a timeless statement. She knew the power of black, especially at a time when young women were cautioned by their mothers that it made them look too old. This is not too old. The black capris were the standard length for the fifties. The length and fit stayed relatively unchanged for over a decade. The above-the-ankle cut looked dreadful once pantlegs dropped below the ankles in the late sixties. But in the eighties it's deemed acceptable again . . . or at least an option. In fact, everything but the soutache-trimmed black velvet slippers (part of the fifties' new at-home style) looks as terrific today as it did twenty-five years ago. (Larry Edmunds)

clothes. We wanted to *be* her. Men may have wanted their women to look like Marilyn Monroe or Sophia Loren. We wanted to look like Audrey Hepburn. She verged on anorexia (we called it skin-and-bones back then). Most men scoffed at the thought of her being sexy. That didn't deter us. It was an inner vision. We saw a princess; men saw a scrawny girl.

She caught our attention in 1953, wearing black capris and a boy's shirt tied at the waist. We called her pixie, elfin, gamin. While other movie stars would come along and be called gaminlike, Audrey was always the ultimate, the original gamin.

If she cut her hair into a short pixie cut, we did too. It didn't

Audrey Hepburn favored black whether she was playing a gamin or the worldly Holly Golightly. Here, as Holly, she wears "the perfect little black dress." It defines the less-is-more approach to dressing. The hat, we were forced to admit, was rather outlandish. But Holly could carry it off—as well as a foot-long cigarette holder. (Paramount Pictures Corporation)

matter that we lacked her doe eyes to balance it. We'd simply repencil our eyebrows to make up for the lack. If only we could imitate that voice too . . .

She wore simple clothes superbly—capris and boat-neck tops, "little" dresses. Restrained lines, refined shapes. In *Funny Face,* the quintessential Hepburn fix, she wore costume after costume, and we drooled over all of them: white pants, white bolero, and a pink cummerbund worn as she fished in the Seine; the satin gown when she flew down the stairs in the Louvre, in front of the Winged Victory of Samothrace, commanding Fred Astaire to "take the picture, take the picture." But best of all—most copyable of all—she wore black tights and turtlenecks. That, we felt sure, was the "real" Audrey Hepburn, that pixie in the bookstore, that undiscovered model. The beatniks extolled the look (or rather, nonlook), but Audrey legitimized it. Black tights, black turtleneck, and a trench coat—that's what we wanted to wear to knock around in, even though we were doing our knocking around in Levittown instead of on the Left Bank. Audrey may have preferred the creations of Givenchy in her private life, but she made the beatnik look respectable, workable, elegant.

She also raised the little black dress to an art form. She taught us how to wear it once and for all, not with fussy fucshia print scarves, but with simple pearls, a black hat, and—did we dare?—a long black cigarette holder.

Years later, in a Sunday magazine story on the Audrey Hepburn look, she was quoted as saying: "My color lacks definition. I prefer to wear black, white or muted colors such as beige or soft pinks or greens. Those colors tend to make my eyes seem darker." She claimed that the only jewelry she owned was pearl earrings and the only gloves, three-quarter-length white ones. Then she offered four rules for the Hepburn look: (1) Look for simple lines. (2) Buy quality rather than quantity. (3) Wear sports clothes that look lived in rather than brand-new. (4) Try to wear the right thing at the right time. But even if we had followed these precepts religiously, we wouldn't have turned into Audrey Hepburn look-alikes.

Despite all the photo sessions, all the interviews, all the careful scrutiny of her walk, her talk, her wardrobe, Audrey Hepburn remained inaccessible, remote, just like the characters she played. She was, in the final analysis, all form and no content.

Audrey Hepburn was still the epitome of elegance, every teenage girl's ideal, but not an attainable goal. We turned to *Seventeen* magazine for a more realistic dream girl. Carol Lynley would do just fine. The model teenager. She smiled at us from Clearasil ads, and we knew that she fretted over pimples too. *Life* magazine, in a day-in-the-life-of-Carol-Lynley story, showed her with rollers in her hair, chatting with her mother, buying furniture with her family—just like us, only she happened to be famous. She was wearing a sleeveless gingham dress with a wide white belt. Why, we had dresses just like that. She projected the image of what we hoped we were or could possibly be. She sold us quite a bill of goods: ointments, knee socks, Jonathan Logan dresses, Bobbie Brooks separates. You name it, she modeled it. She modeled it, we wanted it. What looked good on Carol would look good on us.

Carol Lynley could sell us anything—baby doll pajamas, sundresses, even Ship 'n Shore blouses. Not that we needed much prodding with the Ship 'n Shores. These blouses typified the fifties sporty look—the finely pointed collar turned up to complement an Italian haircut, maybe even with a button open at the neck. We might fill in the neck with a garrote-tied scarf. We snapped up Ship 'n Shores. At $2.98 and $3.98 we would have been fools not to. We never thought of them as budget wear as we do today. They were a brand we knew and relied on for tailoring and value. After all, we were only after cotton broadcloth shirts with simple sleeve variations, in pastels, polka dots, and stripes. Ship 'n Shore represented competence. The working-class dream was a closet filled with Ship 'n Shore tops, all freshly starched and pressed. Every blouse could be worn with a black skirt or capris. Add white shorts in the summer for the sleeveless models. Simple and predictable. Too much so for the eighties. The lure of crisp clean shirts is almost lost on us. With easy-care synthetics and a washer and dryer in every pot, a clean, unwrinkled shirt is effortlessly maintained. A $2.98 Ship 'n Shore white cotton broadcloth shirt was still a status symbol to us in the fifties by virtue of the labor it took to keep it washed, starched, and pressed. Most Ship 'n Shores probably spent half their lives in the vegetable bins of refrigerators, damp and waiting for the iron.

Dan River was another reliable name for clean, smart cottons, especially in plaids. Dan River ads touted their Cinderella frocks, a line of fussy girls' dresses (mostly plaids with demure bows at the waists), as being "never iron." The copy proclaimed, "Some mothers just hang them on the line and let the breezes iron them smooth." That's when mothers spent their days at clotheslines in backyards. Ah, suburbia.

Cotton broadcloth, whether Ship 'n Shore or Dan River, made

This Donna Reed look-alike played Gidget's mother. Is this her housework outfit—freshly pressed shirtwaist, tight belt, and high-heeled pumps? Perhaps so; she isn't wearing gloves, so we know she isn't going out. (The sampler on the wall reads: "To be a real woman is to bring out the best in a man.") (Columbia Pictures Corporation)

up most of our summer wardrobes. It was the perfect fabric for full-skirted shirtwaists of the Donna Reed school of housewifery, and indeed most women wore these dresses. Perhaps not a fresh one every day, perhaps not with heels and starched apron when they did the dusting, but they snapped them up. Shirtwaists and suburbia were made for each other. The hem didn't rise up when you reached for a clothespin, the skirts let you straddle the bed when you made it.

Gingham shirtwaists were new in the spring of 1950. We added gingham to our growing list of uniforms. Its country-fair–Americana look made it popular for years, for dresses, shirts, playsuits, everything.

If the skirts of the fifties shirtwaists, gingham or otherwise, seemed to be five-plus yards around, the sheath seemed less than one. The tighter, the straighter, the better. The narrowest hemline was recorded in *Life* magazine when Dorian Leigh, the top model of those years, posed in a "pared-down" sheath with a sixteen-inch hem. Posed is probably all she was able to do. Walking would be out of the question. That's eight inches across the front and eight inches across the back. Didn't it take more than sixteen inches to go around both her knees?

Sheaths, not the sixteen-inch kind but of a more tolerable width, were easiest to walk in when the hemline ended close to the knees. With a kick pleat, a real, functioning one halfway up the thigh, women could actually stride. But with straight skirts that ended at midcalf, the kick pleat was strictly decorative. When the top of the pleat ended at knee level, it was useless. What should have been the widest part was the narrowest.

However, even if we had to walk like geisha girls, we liked sheaths. They revealed the curves that shirtwaists and crinolines held as closely as state secrets. On the right hips, they were dynamite, worn with high-heeled, wiggle-generating pumps. Sheaths were sexy.

In 1953, *Life,* doing a fashion layout on college date dresses, warned coeds against "slim sheaths, which are not only considered too mature, but are far too confining for dances like the bunny hop." *Life*'s solution to what to wear to the hop: plaid taffetas and Italian brocades, modeled by high school seniors who looked as if they were at least thirty years old.

Despite such matronly missteps, the fifties marked the beginning of the fashion industry's paying attention to younger fashions. Before then, children were "clothed," and teenage girls dressed either as junior versions of their mothers or in the strictly defined collegiate look: pleated plaid skirts, socks, and loafers. Baby boomers became subdeb boomers in the late fifties. Manufacturers began competing to attract preteen dollars. There were more ten-year-old girls than at any time in history (what a grim thought), and their parents were willing to spend more money to dress them. Perky sailor dresses, straw hats for junior-sized heads, black patent shoes, scaled-down gloves. Step right up, little lady. You too can be the belle of the junior high ball, darling of your homeroom.

The subdeb boom then segued into the true teen boom. The *Seventeen* look. Teenage girls had clout (which they achieved by turning whining into a fine art) and Seventh Avenue courted them. Madison Avenue stereotyped them. Ads depicted teenage girls in one pose over and over: upside down, talking on the telephone.

Teen fads were chronicled more closely, from sewing rickrack on sweaters to wearing sword pins. How the two swords were arranged could signal one was "fancy free," "attached," "on the prowl," or "going steady." We were called "date bait." If the term upset us at all in those days, it wasn't because we found it demeaning, but rather that we weren't date bait enough.

When we weren't spending money or talking on the phone, we were dancing. We loved to dance. Alone, with girl friends, with door knobs, and if we were lucky, with boys. We had to consider the danceability of the clothes we wore. We turned to television for guidance. More than Audrey Hepburn, more than Carol Lynley and her *Seventeen* sisters, we were influenced by the girls on *American Bandstand.* They were girls our age who went to real high school in Philadelphia. They called it Philly; we did too. We were Philly-centric in those days. We idolized those kids, who had some-place to go after school—to a TV studio. We went home, changed our clothes, and sat in front of the television set with our geometry books, propped up but ignored, in our laps. It would have been nice to be a Hollywood movie star, nicer to be a New York ingenue model. It would have been nicest to be Justine or Pat, high school girls who got asked to dance *all* the time. We watched their clothes with eagle eyes. Real teenage clothes. The *American Bandstand*

When we were teenagers, the American Bandstand *regulars were our fashion inspiration. The girl in the plaid skirt achieved the perfect fifties silhouette by combining hoop and crinolines. She really knew how to accessorize an outfit: tight belt, white sneakers, and socks. Real chic (which many of us pronounced "cheek"). Tight skirts were another surefire path to popularity and looked most sophisticated with stockings and black flats.* (Dick Clark Company)

girls weren't rich. They bought what we could afford to buy: straight skirts, sweaters, full skirts, princess-line dresses. Never pants. We zoomed in on their footwear. Black flats with stockings, white sneakers with socks. Saddle shoes sometimes. The wrong shoe, or the right shoe with the wrong sock, could break a girl's reputation. We knew it. Justine and Pat knew it. If they wore their socks in a certain way, straight up or triple folded, that assured us it was acceptable.

School sock hops gave us a chance to dance ourselves rather than just watch other people on TV. To toss off our shoes and dance in just our socks with a member of the opposite sex—wow! It was uninhibited. Almost naughty. Parents viewed this as a harmless, meaningless teenage gesture of rebellion. They never understood the meaning behind it. Even we sock hopees weren't conscious of the reason for sock hop excitement. It was provocative to run around without shoes on. It didn't look sexy, all those dirty, stretched-out-of-shape, white-now-black socks, but it felt sexy: sliding around the highly waxed and very slippery gym floor, holding a boy close so you wouldn't fall. Could slipping into satin sheets be any more sensuous? There was an intimacy to dancing in socks that transcended the sloppy sock vision.

What we wore to sock hops was also perfect for bunny hopping (described in *Life* as a dance "done by a line of any number and the eight bar tune is repeated endlessly, until the dancers tire of hopping"). But any of the Latin dances required dressier clothes. The cha-cha-cha, rhumba, and mambo were all sanitized versions of hot tropical rhythms and offered us a break from the bunny hop. The rhumba was best danced in a special rhumba skirt; the ruffled multitiers were perfect for Latin-beat hip action. The mambo was the biggest pre–rock-and-roll dance craze. Imported from Cuba, it spread quickly across the country in 1954 with every conceivable (and many inconceivable) tune mamboized: *St. Louis Blues Mambo, Jingle Bells Mambo, I Saw Mommy Dancing the Mambo.* You didn't need a rhumba skirt for this dance; a full-circle felt one would do. A sexier choice: a skintight sheath and high heels.

Before going somewhere, we would confer with each other by phone: "Are you wearing heels or flats?" To be wearing the only flats in a room filled with heels, or vice versa, meant you were out-of-step. It would ruin the entire evening, cause raised eyebrows and catty remarks.

Lucille Ball wore clunky, high-heeled ankle-strap shoes (black

The twist (as well as the frug and the watusi) was best done wearing high heels and something fringed. The flats of fifties rock-and-roll wouldn't do since they didn't pivot on a dime—crucial for twisting. For those who couldn't afford a new twist ensemble (or had the smarts to know a short-lived fad when it flashed in front of them), fringed belts were available to tie over clothes. (Columbia Pictures Corporation)

suede in particular) in the early fifties, and she is so identified with that period that we think mistakenly that those shoes were the style in heels. Most shoes were less flamboyant (most women were less flamboyant): medium heels and sandals that were conservative, clunkless, rarely as eccentric as Lucy's towering ankle straps.

Dress sandals were surprisingly open and strippy even in the early fifties. Far from clunky, they showed more foot than shoe and were quite graceful. The sandals lost much of their charm, however, at least to our eighties eyes, by being paired with seamed hosiery. (But match up backless fifties sandals with today's seamless pantyhose and you're in business.) Backless sandals and mules were stylish but dangerous to wear. Slippery stockinged feet slid out too easily. Technology to the rescue. In 1954, a new, backless sandal was introduced. A leather and elastic strap was sewn into the arch of the shoe to push the foot forward and keep the shoe in place.

Stiletto heels first appeared in 1952. Dior introduced them and we went wild. Sometimes those French designers are right on target. New developments in metallurgy made the stiletto possible, four-inch spikes of metal-shafted heel. Knock 'em dead. Weapons as well as footwear. Hard to walk in, but so sophisticated. We just had to remember to stay away from gratings and escalators.

Sandals in the fifties were not unlike ones worn today. Capezio and Bernardo have been turning out the same classic styles for thirty years. The most exotic sandals were called gillies: They had black, flat soles with long straps that tied across the foot and up the leg. Apache dancers wore them in those brilliantly choreographed dance numbers in fifties musicals. Espadrilles also had their first go-round back then. Most of the fifties espadrilles had straps that tied around the ankle. Our outlets for creative expression were so limited that we'd spend our time devising new ways to tie them: sometimes across the foot once, then in and out on the side, then around the back and tied in the front. Or tied at the ankle. So many combinations to try.

When we weren't wearing thick white bobby socks, we wore stockings (except in the hottest weather, when going barelegged was acceptable). Stockings were touted as 15 denier, 75 gauge or 15 denier, 60 gauge. Most of us didn't know what in the world a denier or a gauge was, but we did know that the higher the gauge number, the finer the hose. There were walking sheers and dress sheers, dress sheers being easier to run. We felt rich when we had an unopened box of three pairs in our lingerie drawer. They looked so pure, so promising before they were put on the first time. Our mothers told us to put them on wearing gloves so we wouldn't run them.

In the ads, stockings were shown on long legs with plenty of thigh below the brown part. In real life, most of the pasty white thigh was above the stocking. Some stockings ended a mere inch or two above the knee.

Seams were tyrannical. They never stayed straight. To straighten them once they were on was impossible. To do it properly, the whole stocking had to come off and be put on over again. Gloves, please! "Are my seams straight?" we asked over and over, as we clicked our heels together and looked over our shoulders in mock Betty Grable posture.

Our drawers became a jumble of single good, un-run stockings left from pairs, which we tried to match up with other leftovers. It paid to buy the same shade of the same brand again and again. That way you'd never be faced with the embarrassment of not discovering the disparity in leg color until you got to work.

Seamless stockings were available in the early fifties but proved unpopular. They were poorly shaped and snagged easily. Besides, we accepted seams as a way of life. Seams were tedious but not especially ugly. Those dark, shoehorn-shaped reinforcements that ran four inches up the heel—*those* were ugly. But we didn't try to hide them. We wore these stockings with backless sandals, and thought they looked perfectly fine. All the stocking ads in the fifties featured seamed stockings with sandals. Hosiery ads boasted about contrasting heel, toe, sole, and seam being "made especially to wear with open toe shoes." Many fifties styles look pleasing to the eighties eye, but those reinforced-heel, seamed stockings will never cut it again.

When we went barelegged in the summer months, we kept our feet from sweating in our shoes by wearing Peds. Peds were more trouble than seams. Those puckery little foot sacks were supposed to lie in place beneath the shoe line. They never did. Especially not with low-cut Capezios. Sections would puff out here and there and have to be slapped back down. You couldn't slip your feet out of your shoes without having to readjust the Peds all over again. An exposed, Ped-ed foot was much uglier than a naked, sweaty one. Sprinkling talcum powder was a much better solution. White feet weren't a problem unless you left talcum footprints across the rug.

Undergarments remained relatively unchanged from the late thirties through the fifties. Every woman wore a brassiere, a girdle or garter belt, stockings, and a full slip—all in white, except for the stockings. All these items were fussy and detailed beyond necessity. They did the job and then some. There were a few innovations in the fifties: the half slip, the padded bra, and the Merry Widow.

The Merry Widow (such an enchanting name, especially since we were used to the ugliest word in the world, girdle) was an adjunct of the New Look. The new tiny waists needed some trimming, the newly accented bust needed a push upward. The Merry Widow did both. It seemed so womanly. Although first bras were a big event for young teens and came in AA cups, Merry Widows required real breasts—and a formal gown (and a date). The big time. Merry Widows were also worn with New Look suits, but they were fancier than other daytime undergarments. Frothy, lacy, with satin garters, and, most important of all, strapless, there was an element of evening about them. Strapless was daring, tempting gravity as well as men. Part of the upper halves of the bra cups were eliminated, and the corset section pushed the breasts up, giving even an A cup the illusion of an ample bosom.

Bras of the fifties were engineering devices designed to hold the breasts up and out in a basically unnatural position. Breasts were the measure of womanhood. The bigger they were, the more feminine, the more attractive the woman. It was a time of ogling, of Dagmar, Jayne Mansfield, Diana Dors, Marilyn Monroe, Sophia Loren. It was a bad time to be an A cup, and women who lived through those years, stuffed to the proverbial gills, have a difficult time today understanding why flat-chested women choose to go braless.

The fifties ideal was to start off with an impressive pair of D-cuppers, cram them into preformed cones, then aim them toward the moon: uplift and blast-off. British fashion historian Pearl Bender wrote that the ideal bust was "two spiked cones never before seen in Europe and related only to the female form in African sculpture."

In an effort to get a flat piece of fabric to wrap in a cone shape, the bra cups were cut, pieced, and stitched in concentric circles like bull's-eyes. "I dreamed I was an archery target in my Maidenform bra."

Padded bras were deemed a necessity for every woman this side of a C cup. If Mother Nature didn't give us big tits, Macy's could. Padded bra ads filled women's magazines with coy names like "Hidden Treasure" or "Pretender." Foam rubber forms could transform a flat chest into va-va-voom. But there was trouble in paradise. The foam rubber would start to smell, not because it was dirty but because of imperfect technology: The rubber disintegrated over time.

Smell was minor compared with the other debacles that could happen to padded bra wearers. If there was any kind of air pocket between the inside of the foam pad and the outside of the breast, you were a candidate for the world's most humiliating moment. There you were, feeling like a million bucks with an extravagantly padded bra under your new Orlon pullover. Then boom, someone brushed against you and one cup popped inward to fill the space between your nipple and the padding. There you stood, in public, looking like a meteor crater. You couldn't just take the padding by two fingers and pull it out like a piece of lint. There was no graceful way to handle it. You'd have to move to another state where nobody knew you.

Sewn into bras, foam pads were just padded bras, but on their own they were falsies. The ads called them bust pads, but the falsie name persisted. Men called them that. In 1951, the Sears catalog offered twenty-two kinds of falsies, all of them rubber cones in either white or flesh tone. The flesh-colored ones, especially those with nipples, looked like detachable breasts. You could buy round or teardrop-shaped pads or just the nipples alone, "tiny inserts" to "fill out the tips of any bra." Some were aerated with small perforations so your breasts wouldn't sweat as much on hot days, some were covered with satin and lace, but they were falsies just the same.

The only alternative to heavy, smelly foam rubber falsies (other than stuffing your bra with anything that you could wad up from Kleenex tissues to nylons) was the inflated bra. No one ever admitted to actually wearing one, running the risk of having to demonstrate how it worked. Once the bra was in place, the wearer blew through a tiny tube connected to the cup until the "size you always wanted to be" was achieved. Wearing an inflated bra must have generated a great deal of anxiety. At any minute the illusion could literally burst. Perhaps those bras came with instructions to avoid unpressurized planes, aerial tramways, and fast elevators.

Women *always* wore bras. The only exception was when they wore dresses that had their own built-in bras. For dresses that were too low in back to successfully hide even a low-cut Merry Widow, there was a no-bra bra called Bleumette. It was advertised as having "no shoulder straps, no backstrap, no wire, and no hooks"—but plenty of glue. These falsie-type pads came with their own bottles of adhesive and were applied to the lower half of the breast. Somebody must have bought Bleumette bras. They were advertised in all the women's magazines (and still are). But nobody's talking.

We never even dreamed of going without a slip, anymore than going braless. You never knew when you'd be caught between a mad rapist and a lighthouse beacon and the mere outline of your legs would invite ravishment on the spot. Or so our mothers intimated. Full slips were lavished with trim both on the bodice and around the hem. They were made either of lace or had the newest lingerie look—permanently pleated nylon. In really hot weather, a half slip was permissible but only if a blouse was totally opaque. No one wanted to show those ugly bras anyway. Any see-through required a full slip.

Bathing suits of the early fifties seem as overdone and clumsy as the underwear. As undergarments started to look sleeker, bathing suits looked sleeker, because the technology was the same. In the early fifties, the technology was postmedieval. Most suits were one-piece with an excessive amount of boning, lining, and interlining. Nothing was about to show through when wet. It was like wearing an all-in-one corset out in the sun, and just as unflattering. Stretchiness was limited to latex rubber (this was pre-spandex), and often

One step removed from early fifties corset suits, these one-piece bathing suits in Gidget Goes Hawaiian *still had built-in bras and panels.* (Columbia Pictures Corporation)

shirring with latex threads was the best available form. Suits were shirred to a fare-thee-well. The bottom section came in one of two styles: the panel, with a flat section covering the crotch in a smooth sweep from hip to hip; or the dressmaker, a little skirt style that was unfailingly referred to as "figure flattering." If you were thin, it flattered you. If you were fat, it flattered you. But if you had any smarts, you knew that it practically screamed "figure flaw, figure flaw." The panel was better, but neither style was actually in the realm of flattering. Too much modesty and too little technology.

Life showed the bikini bathing suit as early as 1950. It was spelled with a capital B then, and it was still very much associated with the Pacific island where the A-bomb was tested. In fact, the bikini was first called the Atom. The bikini of the early fifties was, from our jaded eighties viewpoint, a very sedate two-piecer. Only in the number of pieces per suit does it resemble today's minimal, high-thigh-cut models. The top was excessively constructed, much like the bras of the time, and the breasts were never exposed. The bottom was as modest as cotton briefs, hugging both the waist and the tops of the thighs. By the end of the fifties, the lower half of the bikini had been modified somewhat. The belly button showed and the proportion between top and bottom was much more flattering. Beachwear—skirts and wraps—became fashion "necessities." Every woman needed a terrycloth shortie robe to throw over her suit.

Playclothes, though strictly for summertime, were as popular then as jogging suits are today. They were one step away from bathing suits, just as demure and relentlessly perky. Most were one-piece, sleeveless top-and-shorts models with matching full skirts, all in cotton broadcloth. Bloomer bottoms on the playsuits were very fashionable, and modest. We looked like thyroid toddlers in them. No one ever asked men if they liked bloomer girls. The bloomer playsuit seemed very practical (until you had to go to the bathroom). Very suburban and so smart with espadrilles.

Women were more concerned with dressing cool in the summer than they are today. Fewer places were air-conditioned. Women never wore long or even three-quarter sleeves in the summer. Generally they wore sleeveless tops with larger-than-necessary armholes that looked very ungainly. Summer outfits were clearly designed to beat the heat. Sleeveless clothes, scoop neck or halter, were all put away on Labor Day.

We were cleverer in one way back then (but this doesn't begin to counterbalance our Spanish infanta complex). We recognized that heavy denim jeans were much too hot for summer. We wore them but only when it was less than 75 degrees outside. Colored (meaning non-navy) and striped denims were an innovation in 1953, and were made into all sorts of sports outfits (wrap skirts and shorts) but not into heavy, skintight jeans. Pedal pushers and shorts seemed a more practical way to dress. Practicality was a much more important consideration than it is today. It seems to have sat out the sixties but played the whole game in the fifties.

Shorts were more practical than prurient. Every woman wore them when it got hot enough. We called them short shorts at the time, and we couldn't possibly imagine them getting any shorter or skimpier. We felt we were knocking on the door of impropriety. But we knocked, at least at first, in the name of staying cool. These waist-hugging shorts (no matter how abbreviated) never revealed the buttocks. Never left you wondering, "If she's wearing any underpants, where could they possibly be?" The underpants under them were modest, wasit-high briefs.

Short shorts were always constructed to hug the top of each leg. No saucy flare to flirt with the disaster of underpants showing. Many had cuffed legs with double-ringed ties at the side to ensure a snug fit. They were as modest as a tight diaper. Yet policemen in White Plains, New York, issued tickets for indecent exposure to women who wore them on city streets. Southhampton, New York, officials issued an ordinance banning the shorts from public "display." Women behaved scandalously when they rolled up the legs a turn or two. That shortened them and tightened them—but still revealed nothing of the hip or buttocks.

Pants were very conventional in the fifties—no bells, no palazzos, no hip-huggers. Silhouettes stayed virtually unchanged for more than a decade: high-waisted, with trim legs, and ending above the anklebone. The zipper was on the side or in the back. A fly front was much too masculine and would draw attention to our crotches.

Pants were classic and long-lasting. They set off brightly colored blouses or bulky sweaters rather than dominated an outfit. The better wool pants were lined. So were some cotton ones. Baggy knees were grotesque, and the lining was meant to keep the knee

*This Jantzen ad from 1954 sums up sportswear in the fifties: short shorts,
Bermudas, and pedal pushers (all cuffed), worn with espadrilles (at $2.49 a
pair!) in coordinated colors and perky Italian hairdos. (Jantzen, Inc.)*

area from stretching. But most lining fabrics were tightly woven, unyielding to a flexed knee. The wool bagged because it stretched to accommodate the bent knee. The lining would rip under pressure. We were often stuck with a perfectly good pair of pants on the outside but shredded-to-smithereens on the inside.

Black capris were the answer to most casual what-to-wear problems. Blouses were tucked in and accessorized with a wide belt. Perfect in photographs. Perfect for the first five minutes after tucking. But there were no belt loops (again, too masculine). Bend over, lean forward, stretch upward, the blouse came untucked, the belt pulled away from the waist. Instant dishevelment. We'd spend our time in compulsive tucking and smoothing. Neatness counted. We could manage to present a neat front to the world, but the rear view was out of the question.

Jeans, too, varied little from year to year. Straight-legged, waist-high denims were often lined with jazzy plaid flannel. Blue jeans, also called dungarees, were worn only for the most casual occasions. A white or plaid blouse, dungarees rolled up to midcalf, thick white socks, and loafers—that was the classic Saturday afternoon outfit. This was long before we faded half the life out of jeans before we'd be seen in public wearing them. We would have laughed at the thought of dry cleaning them.

Fitted capris were only one reflection of our obsession with a figure-revealing fit. It was Queen of Darts time. Every dress, every suit, capris, shorts, and many blouses were darted to death. Long, narrow, triangular darts up from the waist and in from the armpits shaped the bodice of a dress. Darts down to the hips shaped a skirt. Sometimes there were even double rows of darts, up to eighteen in a sheath. No blousing permitted. More shipshape than sexy on most of us.

Darts were formidable. To achieve the ideal fit, they had to point straight to the center of the . . . er . . . um . . . nipple, never acknowledged as such but rather alluded to with phrases such as "in the perfect spot" and "to the fullness of the bosom." Rarely lined up with their charges underneath, most darts ended an inch too low or too high, or offside, or puckering at the tip, looking alarmingly like nipples themselves. Our darted clothes permitted very little variation in weight once we got them fitted properly. Five pounds extra and we looked like a float in the Macy's parade. Five pounds less and the clothes sagged. Anyone who sewed knew exactly how insidious darts were. To get both sides symmetrical and puckerless required master tailoring and the patience of Job.

Thirty years ago, sewing decent-looking clothes was a real skill, and not only because of darts. Zippers were a terror, especially side dress zippers. Hems had to hang properly. Even so-called simple dresses required advanced skills. Fitting and refitting. Ripping and resewing. Sewing today is for simpletons by comparison. Today we use elastic waists, no darts, no zippers, no collars, no cuffs, no plackets, and (our grandmothers would never believe this!) machine-stitched hems. Not so thirty years ago.

Fabrics by the yard were limited, a choice between dowdy and not-too-dowdy. Patterns too. Designers didn't license their creations then. The first company to offer designer patterns was Spadea, at the outrageous prices of seventy-five cents to a dollar. They were ordered through Spadea's newspaper features and proved so popular that *Vogue* started to take notice. Many of *Vogue*'s first batch of designer patterns were by names we had never heard of, but soon every designer with an ounce of business sense was willing to permit home sewers to duplicate creations. At first, patterns were very tricky. Sewing skills—not just A+ in junior high home-ec class, but skills that only years of practice could produce—were required to turn out a creditable Christian Dior and, later, a Jean Muir or an Albert Nipon.

We permitted ourselves a total respite from fit and neatness with one garment: a man's shirt. We borrowed Dad's 17½-35s to wash the dishes, the dog, the car. We tied the tails around our waists. Soon women began to take to men's shirts in a serious way. We didn't just want the nearest male's oversized cast-offs. Sloppy had its limits. We wanted man-tailoring in our sizes. When Brooks Brothers sold to women from their stock of 13–28s, manufacturers wised up and turned out shirts sized for women in pink, small checks, and taffeta. They looked pert and crisp. But the bottom line was—more ironing.

We spent a lot of time ironing in the fifties. Even a pink iron couldn't mask the drudgery. Our mothers impressed the phrase "bandbox fresh" in our minds. We liked our clothes clean, starched, and wrinkle-free. We loved white blouses. But those snowy-white shirts represented a good hour's work for each wearing. When manufacturers started making ruffled blouses in Dacron in 1956, we were warned that they would not be as crisp as cotton. Crispness be damned. Forget crisp, forget the coolness of cotton. So what if nylon turned gray. We were converts.

Dacron was just one of the new man-made fabrics that we were infatuated with in the fifties. Our first fling was with nylon. Available for years but only in drab colors, nylon suddenly showed up in bright colors and light weights. Every ad reminded us that it dried in less than an hour. What more could we want? We never stopped to consider the breathability of fabrics. Our heads were turned by the easy-care qualities of synthetics. *Vogue* rhapsodized about the new nylon lingerie, "found wonderful because of its famous lightness and speed in drying and because it is now so enchantingly pretty." To show just how light a nylon girdle was, *Vogue* photographed one on a scale with a mere half dozen roses to balance it. What freedom, a three-ounce girdle!

Synthetic summer dresses were ballyhooed as better than cotton. Better meant easy care, not easy wear.

Orlon, introduced in 1952, was the first acrylic fiber on the market. It turned up in everything from sweaters to skirts. It could be permanently pleated (the perfect white skirt) or knit. Over seventy million Orlon sweaters were sold in the first four years they were on the market. *Life* proclaimed that "despite the luxury look, they can be washed with little more trouble than nylon stockings." Orlon was strictly a white and pastel phenomenon. It repelled water, which precluded using dark dyes. Orlon's "only flaw," according to *Life,* was that it "set up small electrical charges." The solution, according to a designer the magazine consulted, was "moving slowly." *Life* neglected to warn us against going out in a thunderstorm in our new Orlon duds.

We were so charmed by synthetics that we turned up our noses at cotton. Our old standby was passé. We weeded cotton out of our wardrobes as quickly as possible.

Necklines were fussier a quarter century ago. Often as not, they were in a contrasting color to the dress. White collars, by far the most popular, were basted in so they could be removed quickly. You could wear a dark dress a number of times, but if you were fastidious, you wore the white piqué collar only once.

Collars framed the face and neck, as if we were always ready to have our pictures painted. There were round portrait collars that ended in a sedate midbosom V. Then there were boat necks (the sophisticates among us called them bateau). The boat shape itself was fine, but layering a collar, especially a detachable one, over it was irksome. Collars were impossible to arrange under sweaters and coats. Sabrina necklines, made famous (if a neckline can actually be considered famous) by Audrey Hepburn, were bateau-shaped with bows accenting each shoulder. Cowl collars were soft, draped in folds around the shoulders, and best in wool jersey. Peter Pan collars were perfect for sweater necklines (and we could get them under a coat). Piqué would do for everyday, perhaps with a bit of lace. Angora was much better. We felt like little angels in angora collars. They summed up everything we thought we should be: soft, frivolous, luxurious. Some angora collars had two little pompons attached to cords that tied in the front. Of course, the ultimate collar was mink, or so we read in the magazines. Fur collars were luxury items. If we didn't get them as Christmas presents, we didn't get them at all. Mostly, we didn't get them at all. But we imagined how stylish one could look on an angora sweater or a winter coat.

Some fifties coats, like the polo coat, look as good to us thirty years later as they did then. Others, like brocade dusters, look ridiculous. The polo coat (also called the boy coat) was the most wonderful wrap. Its classic styling sold well in college shops, suburban shops, and city shops. It looked rich. Cashmere was best; camel's hair, acceptable. The polo coat was a safe choice. We could be pretty sure it would look good for years to come. For high school girls, college coeds, and suburban car poolers, the polo coat was the coat of choice. But to maintain our fashion image, we had to re-

The fifties coat, worn by Natalie Wood in Rebel Without a Cause, *had a big shawl collar, dolman sleeves pushed up to the elbow, and no buttons. Hence its nickname, the clutch coat. With its full hemline, we could sashay forth day or night. Very few fifties coats had that versatility, or so we thought.* (Warner Brothers)

member it turned into a fashion pumpkin when the sun went down.

To go "out" after dark, we needed an evening coat. What to wear over cocktail dresses was a constant concern. How many of us have evening coats today? In the fifties, a separate, dressy coat was a wardrobe necessity. If it would look totally out of place in the day-time, then it was a perfect evening coat. Fashion magazines offered pages of them to choose from in taffeta, moiré, brocade in full duster styles. A good dousing of Lenthéric and we could face the world, transformed from daytime drudge into dancing darling.

Summer evenings required dressy shawls or stoles. Not only knitted and crocheted, stoles could also be flat weave, ideally out of the same fabric as the dress. One of the most absurd fads of the early fifties was organdy coats. Sheer and stiff, with all French seams, these dusters were touted as special summer evening wraps.

The shawl-collared cashmere coat was one fifties coat that could pass muster both day and night. As it had no buttons to keep it closed, we started calling it the clutch coat. It was at its most grand with the sleeves pushed up near the elbows and long gloves tucked underneath. Again—eminently sashayable.

Two types of short coats, not jackets but regulation coats, were big sellers in the fifties: toppers and car coats. Toppers, often inelegantly worn with full skirts, were springtime favorites in light-colored wools. Perfect for Easter.

Car coats were a product of the great move to the suburbs. The Levittown look was never sophisticated, never elegant, but so practical. The same women who raved about Dacron shirtwaists raved about car coats. One of the best-selling styles had a back belt below waist level. They looked best worn with capris, but all too often were paired with shirtwaists.

Raccoon coats were an aberrant one-season fad in the fall of 1957. Suddenly, mysteriously resurrected from attic trunks, 1920s vintage raccoon coats were put on sale in department stores for $25. Some were worn and moth-eaten, but they sold anyway. New raccoon coats, more stylish, sold briskly for many times that amount. Full-length raccoon coats came and went quickly, like foraging animals in the night. By fall 1958, raccoon was strictly for collars, to be tacked onto loden cloth car coats.

Jumpers were new in the mid-fifties—if anything adapted from the garb of medieval pages can be considered new. We lauded their versatility. Take a simple black wool jumper, for example. You could wear it to the office with a Lady Hathaway shirt underneath for the perfect Katie-Gibbs-approved secretarial look. Duck into the ladies' room at 5:00 P.M., whisk off the blouse, and you were ready for a night on the town in a legitimate little black dress. There was no need to worry about perfume. Many ladies' rooms had dispensers that would spray you with a shot of perfume: five cents for Tweed or Yardley English Lavender, ten cents for Chanel No. 5 or Tabu.

What we bared and what we didn't was clearly, universally understood and adhered to. Shirts remained buttoned up so that slips and bras would never be revealed. V-necks suggested seduction, but were never V-ed so low as to show any real cleavage. Plunging necklines sounded more provocative than they actually were.

Low necklines were considered better in back. We loved the back. We even buttoned our cardigans there, if we had someone to help us dress. Scoop backs came down almost to bra level (occasionally for a daring scoop, a low-cut Merry Widow was called into service). Necklines in back were quite fussy too, with detachable collars and bows that made sitting back in chairs irritating. In 1953, *Life* recommended low-backed cocktail dresses, especially in black, for a "public grown jaded on strapless tops and plunging necklines, the exposed back is back for evening."

Spaghetti straps were an acceptable level of bareness in the summer. No one dared to wear them without a strapless bra.

Midriffs could be exposed, but only above the waist. No hip-huggers, ever. Exposing three inches above the navel was flirtatious but acceptable. Three inches below was whorish. Shorts and bathing suits always hugged the upper thigh. Never, ever did we reveal an inch of hip. The hip and the thigh were two separate entities, one to be revealed, one to be covered. No high rise. We thought it looked ugly. Our underpants wouldn't have permitted it. Nor would our mothers have.

In 1957, clothes seemed to open up. Looser shapes, bulky sweaters, blanket-plaid skirts, short boots, pendants instead of circle pins—suddenly fashion turned a corner. We didn't throw out our wardrobes, not our beloved shirtwaists and sundresses, but new purchases reflected a newly relaxed style.

The chemise was the bellwether fashion of the late fifties. This style was introduced in Paris by both Balenciaga and Givenchy, reportedly working independently. The graceful couture chemise dresses, whose seemingly unstructured long torsos were carefully shaped to flow smoothly with body movements, were both quickly and clumsily copied in the U.S. These knock-offs were finally spurned by American women.

The chemise was the source of many jokes in 1958. "Those balloon dresses look like the girls have the designers inside the dresses with them," chortled Earl Wilson. While the designers called them chemises, people in the street called them sacks, bags, or the shoplifter's delight.

The sack was too radical. It hid the bustline and the waist completely, and it left women with nothing to accentuate but the hips. Most women didn't want that. They could give up waist cinchers for a fitted bodice but not for fitted hips. The first sacks had a lot of back detailing with fullness of fabric gathered at the fanny, which was often emphasized with a bow. Wide belts, frequently in black patent leather, were slung on the hips. They were practically the same belts that women had been wearing around their waists, only now they were thirty-six inches long instead of twenty-four inches. Women shuddered. The worst of the chemise styles was a sort of cocoon with a puffy middle and a skintight skirt. When the chemise was brought out a second time in 1960, much of its belated success had to do with eliminating the cocoon shape and permitting the dress to skim over the total body. It was more shift than sack.

Seventh Avenue manufacturers betted heavily on the chemise and lost. We talked about it. We joked. We all bought *one.* At one point, 80 percent of all moderately priced dresses sold were sacks. The working girl's drop-dead outfit, for a few weeks anyway, was a sack dress, usually in a shantung-like fabric, perhaps the new synthetic Cupioni. The dress had a white collar and a bow at the base of the spine (because it often buttoned down the back too) and a low belt. It was worn with basic black pumps. (Some revolutions can be meted out in stages.) Women were told that buying a sack would help fight inflation, a patriotic gesture. Fashion experts advised that the chemise had to be worn at the proper length, just below the knee. Longer was dowdy. If we didn't like the look, surely it was because we were wearing the chemise too long.

Men hated it. Marilyn Monroe wore one. Men loved her, hated her sack. It was the subject of newspaper editorials, always against. Adlai Stevenson denounced the sack as Russian propaganda designed to cause confusion within our ranks.

In Birmingham, Alabama, bonfires were set to burn the garment. Placards read: "Bring Back Curves" and "Sack the Sack"—all duly recorded by *Life*. In Tuscaloosa, Alabama, high school boys declared their own civil war. When 150 girls showed up at school wearing sack dresses, it was too much for the southern males to take. As self-appointed protectors of southern femininity, they had to make a statement, to show the ladies the error of their judgment. The boys showed up at school with their shirttails hanging out. See, girls, this is just how sloppy you look. The principal, a member of the two-wrongs-don't-make-a-right school of thought, ordered the shirts tucked in.

Dior's trapeze, a close cousin to the chemise, was more successful in its first U.S. go-round, also in 1958. The trapeze flared from under the fitted bosom into a triangular skirt, almost skimming the body at the waist but deftly hiding hips and thighs. Emphasizing the bosom and the rib cage was almost as good as emphasizing the waist, and women bought the dress.

Sack dresses stayed around for a few months. Then they disappeared. There were no sacks in 1959, unless you were a year behind things. For the first time, women as a collective consumer force told Seventh Avenue that they were not willing to wear just anything. Perhaps manufacturers should be more selective than slavish in their cheap Parisian knock-offs.

Mostly we went back to presack dress styles. Full-skirted sundresses all summer. Jumpers for school and office. Pleated skirts and blazers. School styles were tailored shirts and skirts, socks and loafers. Boys couldn't really perceive any more curves, more definition, but they thought they could. The masculine prerogative of girl-watching was restored.

The chemise had shortened skirts to accommodate its basic

gracelessness, and that just-below-the-knee length stayed popular in 1959, no matter what the style.

We got a hint of things to come with our introduction to Jackie Kennedy, the wife of the Democratic candidate for President. We had our first real look at her in 1959.

We also got a first glimpse of another beauty whom later on we would all want to look like. Ali MacGraw, then Alice MacGraw, Wellesley '60, was the cover girl in *Mademoiselle* magazine's college issue. She looked clean-cut and clever. She took up where Audrey Hepburn's gamin look left off. And Audrey Hepburn was beginning to dress like Jackie Kennedy.

And now—my life in clothes! My earliest memory of anything to do with clothes on my back is a sort of Delftware-blue dress with a white collar that I had when I was four years old. The primary feature of that dress was three plastic buttons in a vertical row on the front which were in stoplight colors: red, yellow, and green.

—Sara B. Chase

The outfit I remember best is my going away outfit when I was married in 1948. I wore it all through the fifties. The suit was royal-blue gabardine with a short fitted jacket and a very flared skirt. I had three children, and after each child was born, I would wear the suit home from the hospital just to prove I hadn't lost my figure. Needless to say, I also wore a very tight girdle. The suit still hangs in storage in the attic. My twenty-five-inch waist is gone, but every time I look at it I remember those days.

—Joan Padon

We moved to California when I was in the sixth grade (1956). My family had a lot of kids and we couldn't always afford the latest fashions. My older cousin made a hoop for me out of wire coat hangers twisted together. Unfortunately, I wasn't up on all the techniques of wearing a hoop and my first experience with it was in crowded quarters, negotiating the aisle of the school bus, at which time the ends of two hangers disconnected and my hoop went totally awry. After suffering intense humiliation, I tried it one more time. Going between the desks in the classroom, I suffered the same consequences. I went to the girls' rest room at recess and took the damn thing off and threw it away. So much for high fashion!

—*Michele Burgess*

In junior high, 1955–1956, multiple petticoats were in full swing, so to speak. I remember trying to convince my mother that three or four of these were barely a decent minimum. It was critical that the skirt stand out like a longer version of the ballerina's tutu. As I recall, there were two kinds of petticoats: the net one which scratched your legs and the cotton lace, all seven or eight yards of which had to be ironed.

One day I lost my bottom petticoat. Of course, it was one that was really ratty and probably, knowing me at the time, not real clean. It had a button at the waist which apparently came off. As I began walking out of class, there was this ratty petticoat draped about my feet. I was paralyzed with embarrassment, and around me boys were snickering. The homeroom teacher was male, of course. The boy walking behind me—who undoubtedly had sisters—calmly bent down, untangled my legs from the petticoat, handed it to me, and walked out. I spent the next two periods or so in the girls' room—dying.

—*Gloria Casvin*

In the fifth grade, 1957, full skirts hit. The fuller, the better. So we wore not one, not two, but three or more petticoats, starched stiff. When that wasn't enough, we learned to wear a hoopskirt. I say learned because it took practice to learn to seat yourself without the hoop flying up in front of you. I remember my mother suggesting that I *could* wear just one petticoat. Couldn't I see how much more graceful it looked, wearing just one? Of course not. What was the point of wearing just one? The fuller, the better. The beginning, for me, of extreme styles, of sacrificing comfort for design. For the next ten years, I would eagerly follow almost every new fad, no matter how strange.

—*Lyn Messner*

The bottommost layer was stiff net and resulted in symptoms akin to poison ivy as we scratched our way through the day.

—*Linda Dahl*

Conformity, thy name is teenager! When we sought fashion inspiration from American Bandstand, we were presented with a unified front. The lesson here: bouffant hairdos, bouffant skirts. Fussy, frilly, and oh-so-feminine. No variation in skirt length, little difference in shoe style. The second girl from the right looks like she's having a hard time bucking the tide. There's nothing really wrong with her outfit, but she'd have been less dorky-looking in a full-skirted pastel number. (Dick Clark Company)

Any one of these crinolines would make a skirt stand out nicely. Two, three, or all four would look even better. The nylon number at the lower right had one hundred yards of netting in it. (Sears, Roebuck and Company)

There's "9 whirling yards of taffeta" in this acetate teen skirt, "almost twice a full circle." It's hard to figure how that fit around a twenty-two-inch waist; that's a twenty-seven-to-two ratio. The Los Angeles edition of this Sears catalog called the skirt "dramatic date bait." Those were innocent times. Nothing this side of a Fredericks catalog is billed as dramatic date bait these days. (Sears, Roebuck and Company)

"Stand-out" petticoats are what I called them. Those horribly stiff, scratchy net things my mother thought were so necessary but were the epitome of discomfort. I had to wear them to church under my Sunday dresses. Before I would sit down in the pew, I would reach behind me and under the petticoats, lift them up almost to the height of my head, and sit down—bare legs against cold pew. I'm sure it looked pretty odd, but there was no way I was going to sit on three or more layers of scratchy netting for an hour.

—*Pamela J. Baergen*

I ironed some of my petticoats with wax paper to stiffen them, and starched everything that could be starched. The feel of those crinolines was simply heavenly. I think in West Virginia we all felt just like Scarlett O'Hara, and I particularly liked having my small waist emphasized as I was getting fairly plump in the hips at that point.

—*Sara B. Chase*

I would wear two or three slips at a time. When I washed them I would dip them in a starch solution and then set them out to dry. Then I would iron them with spray starch so that they would be even fuller.

—*Eileen Fond*

My favorite crinoline was one made of two layers of pink net that could be pulled apart for volume so it didn't need starching so often.

—*M. Miller*

There was a girl in my school—a real sosh—who always wore her hoopskirt with such aplomb. She'd sashay down the aisles between the desks (to sit with a boy! in the eighth grade!) without it once ever flipping up. Not even the school bus was her undoing like it was for the rest of us "mere mortals." And the ridge of her hoop never showed through her skirt either. Not showing the hoop line was like not having VPL today. She must have topped her hoop with layers of crinolines. She wore all this very long and with *real* Capezios.

—*Ellen Ekman*

On a trip to Niagara Falls in 1959 (three adults and two children), we packed tightly to fit in all the luggage. However, the dresses I had packed necessitated some sort of crinoline underneath which was absolutely essential to a twelve-year-old girl. Not only were two crinolines placed on our suitcases in the car trunk, but a hoopskirt as well. Every time my father opened the trunk, my slips would pop out.

—Ginger Hill

In junior high, 1959 or so, I remember wearing two or three crinolines at a time and being so hot and itchy from all the net. Then styles went to the other extreme of being very tight, straight skirts with kick pleats. Even girls weighing under one hundred pounds, as I did, had to wear girdles as part of the fashion.

—Linda Finch

My first day of high school in 1962, I wore so many crinolines, my skirt stood straight out. I remember counting them in the girls' bathroom with my friends to see who had the most. My hair was a big bouffant. Oh, it was horrible! I thought I looked so great. At the time, I *knew* everyone looked at me because I looked so good. Now, I wonder . . .

—Sherry Alberoni

The hoop slip was never fun. It was breezy and one had to be very careful when taking a seated position so that the skirt did not pop up in one's face.

—Carolyn Zucker

Brand-new or freshly starched tulle petticoats snagged nylon stockings at knee level like mad, rendering nylons unwearable. That made nylons an even more precious commodity because your mother wouldn't buy you replacement ones.

—Nancy Kinney

Crinolines itched and those hoopskirts made sitting a problem until you got the hang of lifting the rear up before you sat down.

—Sandy Whitehurst

When I was ten, I had a mambo skirt. It was lavender felt, a full circle, with footprint directions for the mambo across the front. Lavender was considered a daring color then.

—Ellen Ekman

From my earliest recollections of pink dresses and patent leather shoes, clothes were important to me. My early years were at the end of an era when clothes symbolized steps in growing up—boys wearing their first long pants and girls wearing girdles (or should I say foundation garments) and nylon stockings. Though we weren't exactly poor, day-to-day life was not very glamorous or necessarily luxurious, and growing up represented attaining status (children in those days were seen and not heard). It was nebulously implied that growing up also included the longed-for luxuries of life. We could hardly wait!

Clothes also represented status to us that the modes of dress drastically separated the educated and the noneducated, the "blue collar" worker and the "white collar" worker success story, and we wanted desperately to be identified with the next higher standard of living. So we "wouldn't be caught dead" without the right shoes or matching bags, or wearing white after Labor Day, or without hats and gloves.

—Nancie L. Porter

In elementary school I always wore dresses. Dresses were for school. It never occurred to me or anyone else to have the girls wear pants, despite skinned knees and later being inhibited on the playground because of wearing a skirt. It wouldn't be until after I graduated from high school in 1965 that girls would begin to wear pants to school.

—Lyn Messner

My mother is a former grade school teacher. She always dressed my sister and me in white blouses and dark (navy and plaid) skirts. I don't know for sure but it seems like that's all we ever wore to school, year in and year out. I got so completely sick of the same old thing that to this day I do not own a white blouse, anything navy, or nary a plaid anything.

—Annette Swanberg

Nineteen fifty was the year I turned twelve, and at that point (seventh grade, big junior high), clothes became very important to me and my memory of them is clear. We wore white dickey collars or small silk scarves tied in a square Girl Scout knot. I felt snappiest in a navy wool skirt (very straight), burgundy sweater set, white dickey

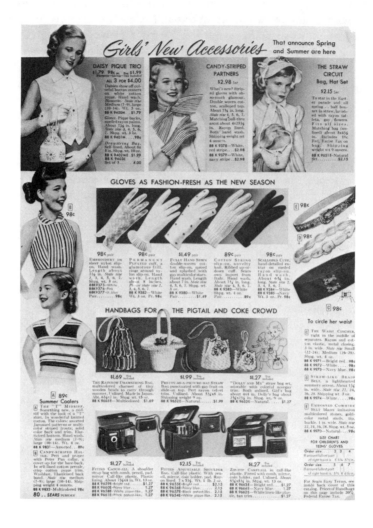

Little girls dressed like little ladies in the fifties. We were taught early that hats and gloves were important dress-up items. Note the "handbags for the pigtail and Coke crowd." Those calflike plastic purses were special prizes. (Sears, Roebuck and Company)

with a tiny cutwork motif, and boxy, navy-and-white small-check jacket.

—*Sara B. Chase*

In junior high, one of my favorite outfits was a full-skirted, scoop-necked black jumper and a white, round-collared, puffy-sleeved blouse which I accessorized with white knee socks and black flats. I thought it was "dreamy." One morning when I was dressed in my dynamite outfit, waiting for the school bus, somebody called me "Alice." I replied that my name wasn't Alice. The boy replied, "Well, you look like Alice in Wonderland." It was the last time I ever wore *that* outfit. I was furious that some dumb boy had ruined it for me. What did he know? Nothing about "Fashion" (as I saw it) and too much about Lewis Carroll.

—*Ellen Ekman*

In the sixth grade, I *finally* convinced my mother to let me have a plaid skirt and sweater. Red, green, and navy plaid and a red pull-over sweater. Up till then it had been dresses, and I felt so babyish. But skirts and sweaters were definitely big girl and, after all, I *was* in the graduating class. We had a lot of boy-girl parties, but it's funny that what I wore doesn't stand out in my mind at all. It's more that skirt and sweater that I wore to school. I guess I remember it because *I*, not my mother, chose it.

—*Susan Stern*

What I chiefly remember about my clothes in the fifties is how formal they seemed. I have a picture of me in 1957, taken on my way to some get-together of senior high girls. If you can believe it, I wore white gloves and a string of pearls. Today such an event among my daughter's friends would produce an entire roomful of blue jeans.

—*Caroline Latham*

While I was a product of the times and the rules were clearly defined and it never entered our heads to question them, or not to go along with them, I think clothes have always meant more to me than to my contemporaries. I could never stand being submerged in a group. Back then, I used clothes as a way of standing out, or attracting attention. I had a desperate need to prove to myself that I wasn't like the rest—that there was something special about me. I designed and made the most dramatic outfits that far surpassed anything that Doris Day ever wore! These were everything from a Scotch outfit, complete with matching scarf and Scotch hat, to color-coordinated ensembles with matching shoes and accessories. I'm sure that many people thought I was a nut, but I assumed their double takes were compliments.

—Nancie L. Porter

I think I can date my specific interest in fashion back to the seventh grade when, in history class, my special project was "The Influence of Travel (the automobile, the train, etc.) on Women's Clothing in the Late Nineteenth and Early Twentieth Centuries." It was with two other girls and we had such a marvelous time. We checked out costume books from the library and drew and drew pictures of clothing. I think we got sort of off the track of travel, we were having so much fun just drawing the clothes.

—Susan Stern

In the fifties there was no emphasis on originality. We bought clothes because they were what everyone else wore. The most important thing was to dress like everyone else. There was no real choice like there is today.

—Emby Searson

In 1958, at my elementary school in California, the big fad for girls was to wear a black skirt, white blouse, colored cardigan, same-colored scarf tied loosely about the neck, same-colored angora socks and a big same-colored fake rose on the left just above the heart. Boy, I had that outfit in every color those roses came in! And same-colored belts turned around backward.

—Michele Burgess

I doubt that the young people of today can imagine a time when girls and women never left the house in anything but a skirt unless it was for play or sports. Even when I took machine shop at Stratford High School, I had voluminous aprons to protect my New Look-length skirts.

—Nancie L. Porter

I was really into looking sexy in high school. *Really* tight, short skirts, fitted blouses, semipointed high-heeled shoes. I never gave any thought to comfort.

—Emby Searson

Back in the fifties, Mother was paying the bills. I loved tight clothes and tight belts and big skirts and high heels. I had to make the skirt absolutely straight so that it cut in or curved under my rear. That was important. You wore these skirts with see-through nylon blouses and tight belts. I remember vague feelings that it was uncomfortable. But it looked right.

—Peggy Byrnes

I liked school uniforms because they cut down on the competition of clothes. But even then, there were individuals! At St. Paul's we wore gray skirts with two pleats, one center front, one center back. The fast girls (even in a Catholic high school, we had fast girls) would stitch down the pleats to midthigh to make them tight skirts. Some girls shortened their skirts too far, so we had to have uniform checks where we knelt down to see if our hems touched the floor. If they didn't, they were too short.

—Rose Mary Kimble

We wore long, straight, tight wool skirts and could hardly climb the stairs. We wore wide waist cinchers (elastic belts), with full felt skirts, sometimes with a felt poodle on one side wearing a collar and chain. Some of us had poodle cuts, which may have been influenced by Mary Martin.

—Anna Lee Fuchs

I never liked straight skirts, either for comfort's sake or how I looked in them.

—Susan Stern

Some of us had mouton coats. Mine was a most prized possession. It was so thickly padded and had such wide shoulders that if two of us wore them, no one else could sit comfortably with us in a car seat.

—Anna Lee Fuchs

Polo coats were called "boy coats" in Milwaukee. I think I told my
mother I would never leave the house "for the rest of my life" if I
didn't have one. Get the picture? It really was a good, warm, comfortable coat in the winter. However, it was popular to buy them
about two sizes (maybe even four) too big and wear them just barely
above the ankles. With that coat in gray, navy, or tan, saddle shoes,
ankle socks, and a babushka (triangular head scarf) on your head—
that was perfection in the fifties.

—*Sandy Whitehurst*

All through college, I wore a camel-colored polo coat with a long
red plaid muffler to which I added, as did we all in West Virginia, a
thick, long red fringe.

—*Sara B. Chase*

In my opinion, Bermuda shorts have been the most enduring
clothing style. Because they are so functional, I have worn them
intermittently from 1955 to today. In the early sixties, plaid,
guaranteed-to-bleed Madras cloth was the height of fashion. I also
remember wearing a length of shorts between short shorts and Bermudas, called Jamaica shorts. They ended at midthigh.

—*Carolyn Zucker*

When I went to school in Andover, Massachusetts, we had to have
striped button-down shirts from Brooks Brothers and mohair crew-
neck sweaters over them, with shirt collars *inside* the sweaters. Wool
skirts and slacks, Argyle socks and penny loafers, English Fog Cut-
ter trench coats.

—*Kelly Lange*

Pedal pushers in the fifties were as common as Levi's are today.

—*Sandy Whitehurst*

I remember loving my dad's shirts when I was a teenager. My
after-school uniform was one of his shirts with jeans. I dyed them
pastels and *loved* them.

—*Regina Neuman*

I especially loved the boned strapless dress for proms. Very sexy.
Only you would move, the dress didn't. My favorite was a navy taf-

The polo coat, aka the boy coat. If it weren't for changing hemlines this coat could last thirty years. No other coat style has enjoyed such incredible popularity. Investment dressing, long term. In the fifties when this coat was offered for sale, it was viewed as too sporty to wear over dressy dresses, but today it is much more acceptable after dark. (Sears, Roebuck and Company)

For teens to matrons, toppers were truly indispensable spring coats. They were not jackets but hip-length coats, usually in a pastel wool. It was a difficult length to wear successfully. Toppers looked tolerable with slim sheaths, but were an abomination combined with full hoopskirted dresses (a fashion sin many of us conveniently forget having committed). (Sears, Roebuck and Company)

Bermuda shorts always looked better from the front than from the rear, even on Doris Day. Though baggy, the look was (and is) classic Ivy League-turned-preppie with tailored shirt, cardigan sweater, and knee socks. (Columbia Pictures Corporation)

These two-piece sets were smart casual wear in the fifties (and are now all the rage in vintage-clothing shops). Jeans were lined with the same plaid or print flannel of the shirts. Zippers were on the side, never fly front. (Sears, Roebuck and Company)

This picture of four seniors at their 1953 high school prom was taken for the local paper's society page. Strapless was everything. Womanhood achieved. Most prom girls subscribed to the you-can't-wear-too-much-tulle school of formal wear. These belles of the ball displayed their corsages with pride (their dates having dutifully consulted the girls' moms as to the appropriate colors). (Anna Lee Fuchs)

feta that eventually turned gray from hanging in a sunny room, but only on one side.

—*Janice Morgan*

I had a burning desire for a white rabbit fur to wear with my white strapless prom gown. My vivid memories are all for things I was either denied or had to save for.

—*Sally Henderson*

Dyed-to-match peau de soie (really just cheap satin) shoes were the only possible footwear solution for a formal occasion. Shoe stores were obliging in matching pastel shades of tulle, then called net, to specification. The gaggiest thing a girl could possibly wear with her formal was lace or net mitts, those fingerless above-the-elbow gloves.

—Nancy Kinney

To the senior prom, 1956 in Massapequa, we wore strapless tops, big long skirts of tulle. Mine was white with four or five tiers of tulle ruffles over crinolines and a hoop. I found out somehow that another girl had bought the same dress. Disaster! But Mother and a neighbor changed it at the last minute with a pink sash.

—Peggy Byrnes

At our high school prom, the nuns had a rule against girls wearing spaghetti-strap dresses. The straps had to be at least one inch wide. (Strapless, never!) My friend Celeste and I had the same dress. It came with spaghetti straps and I had special straps made to regulation. Celeste, who later became a nun, didn't and she got away with it.

—Rose Mary Kimble

The *pièce de résistance* of those high school years was a luscious evening gown I wore to my senior prom and later to a few dances in college. It was very sophisticated for me in those days—black cotton lace over white taffeta, spaghetti straps and all. Nobody else had a black-and-white dress for the prom; everyone had those sticky-sweet, ice cream pastels, and I really like being different than the rest of the pack. I still have this dress. Maybe I'll wear it again someday.

—Annette Swanberg

One could own formal after formal in high school—but to own a BLACK COCKTAIL DRESS was really the last word. Mine was a sheath with an interesting draped neckline, sleeveless, in some wonderful, drapy, crepy fabric. Not low, but off the shoulder somehow. The world was mine when I wore it.

—Nancy Kinney

When I was in high school in Whittier, California, 1953–1957, the big rage was straight skirts, which were wool flannel and fell to the

Come, let's stroll, stroll across the flo-or—for which we needed the perfect strolling outfit. We again turned to our American Bandstand *peers for guidance: straight skirts, sweaters (matching was best), flats (saddle shoes or brown bucks), and thick white socks that were worn straight up.* (Dick Clark Company)

widest part of the calf, definitely unflattering. These skirts were usually gray, navy, or black, and coupled with sweater sets, white bucks, and a buck bag. This was supposed to be *it*. The sweater sets for the "rich girls" were cashmere or angora. They were short-sleeved pullovers and cardigans of the same color, with a little white piqué collar or scarf at the neck. The problem was, you were always concerned about how boys saw you, that you perspired a lot and wrecked the underarms of those precious sweaters. I was always embarrassed because my sweet pink sweaters got grungy armpits, and I knew my mom had paid a lot for them so I could keep up with the cheerleaders.

—Joanna Wood

I genuinely liked sweater sets because they were warm, soft, and came in beautiful colors. The upkeep was another thing. We had to wash them in cold water with Ivory Flakes, nothing else (no Woolite then). First we ran a little warm water to melt the flakes, then we added cold water. We washed the sweaters, rinsed them forever, and then wrung them out in a Turkish towel, blocked and laid them flat to dry. Lots of sweaters took lots of time. If you were lucky enough to have cashmere sweaters, they all had little pearlized buttons the same color as the sweater.

—Sandy Whitehurst

In winter I wore sweater sets. I had them in almost every color except baby blue, and I had little clips to hold the cardigan in place on my shoulders when I didn't have my arms in my sleeves. These clips were an early lesson in nonfunctional fashion. I loved the look but seldom used them. When I tried, my cardigan quickly slipped off my shoulders altogether, the chain between the clips rode high on my neck, and I looked like some sort of sweater-set Superwoman with my cardian flying along behind me. The clips wound up in my drawer.

—Rochelle Reed

Buttoning cardigans in the back was very popular in the fifties. It was like a second life for your sweater.

—Sandy Whitehurst

There was a real snob sweater hierarchy. To have a sweater set was to own the world. A cashmere or lambs' wool or angora set, the height of chic, was simply unattainable to most high school girls. An Orlon set sufficed. Ban-lon and Tycora sweaters appeared in the late fifties. When their novelty wore off, they were deemed the bottom of the line.

Buttoning any cardigan up the back was cute at first, but later was symbolic of being too poor to own a regular pullover.

—*Nancy Kinney*

Angora sweaters will always be *verboten* to me because of the time I wore a new yellow one to a dance and it rubbed off all over my date's black sweater.

—*Rochelle Reed*

To be really cool in high school, we bought lettermen's sweaters long enough so that we could put our hands in the pockets and still keep our arms straight.

—*Rose Mary Kimble*

My mother sent away for a gadget guaranteed to keep your blouse neatly tucked inside your skirt. It turned out to be a piece of elastic with a hook to close it but it worked well. Sometimes it rode up a little when you bent over and you could see it in the back. It looked like some piece of elastic from your underwear had gotten loose. One time, the leftover bit of elastic in the front, about three inches of it, got loose and flopped over the front of my skirt without my knowing it. Some dumb boy pointed to it and said, "What's that?" I was mortified. How could I explain? A boy would never understand.

—*Ellen Ekman*

During the fifties it was imperative that each postpubescent American female have a "little black dress" in her closet. This was usually a straight-skirted, nondescript garment that could be dressed "up" (with fake pearls) or "down" (with a multicolored scarf) and was worn *ad nauseam* by those of us who could never decide what to wear. I always had a black dress. One time it was a black linen sheath, another time it was a black jersey scoop neck, high in the front and low in the back. My mother would tell me that a sixteen-year-old girl shouldn't wear black, but I did. And I'd put my hair in a French twist so I'd really look sophisticated.

—*Carolyn Zucker*

In Alabama there were secret dress rituals that, as a new student in school, I stumbled across only when I made some egregious mistake.

Like wearing red on Friday. That meant you had "gone all the way." Imagine the terror of getting on the school bus in the morning wearing a red sweater and, after much chuckling and whispering, someone telling you what sin you had committed. I was stuck for the whole day. No way I could go home and change and explain *that* to my mother. Green on another day meant you were gay (or "homo," as it was called then, and there).

—Ellen Ekman

In high school the biggest fashion influence in my life was Alexandra, the older sister of my best friend. She was out of college and working as an assistant buyer at Saks Fifth Avenue in Detroit. She'd come home in thirty-dollar cashmere sweaters! Forty-dollar shoes! Such extravagance. She always had a classic style. The latest and the best. She made a lasting impression on me about buying quality and classic.

—Gloria List

Both my sister and I got one pair of "school" and one pair of "dress" shoes each year. We always waited until the second week of school in the fall to see what the other kids were wearing. I guess this was our follow-the-crowd phase. Actually, the shoes always turned out to be Buster Brown oxfords anyway.

—Annette Swanberg

White bucks. I would put baby powder into a powder puff bag and carry it around with me at school all day and keep touching up the smudge marks.

—Eileen Fond

We carried our buck bags to polish or to add a little white powder to our white buck shoes, which looked like oxfords, during the lunch hour or after P.E.

—Joanna Wood

In the fifties the status symbol was the Joyce shoe, that white-laced wedgie that by today's standards would be considered an ortho shoe only nurses might wear. You just weren't in unless you clomped your way into class with your Joyces, which had to be worn with thin white bobby socks. Even the blue and white box they came in was a prized possession.

The cleaning ritual was as important as the shoe itself. Sunday night, after we did the dishes, we would get out the Shinola and carefully polish our Joyces until they were spotless. Then we soaked the laces in Clorox, hung them to dry, and come Monday morning, we climbed aboard the school bus, careful not to put any scuff marks on those beauties. That rather ugly, clunky leather wedgie brought confidence, acceptance. You belonged.

—Ailene Watson

I had white loafers and carried a "bunny bag" to smack the smears with at all times. Bunny bags (I think shoe stores sold them or gave them away when you bought a pair of white shoes) were little two-inch-square pouches of porous fabric filled with a chalklike dust. You'd take the bunny bag out of its case and hit it against your shoe and chalk would come out.

—M. Miller

Blue-and-white oxfords. I hated polishing the white part, as I would get white polish on the blue part and then it looked tacky. But I'd wear them anyway, since I never did have blue polish and it never occurred to me to get any.

—Eileen Fond

My first pair of pumps were called Cuban heels. Squatty, maybe just a little more than an inch high. Just enough not to be flat. They were clunky and ungraceful, and since many of us had full-grown feet and half-grown bodies, they made us look even more awkward. But if we realized that, we kept our mouths shut. We weren't old enough for high-heeled pumps and didn't want to go back to flats.

—Ellen Ekman

I got my first pair of real heels in the eighth grade. They had metal tips and you could hear me coming three blocks away.

—Rose Mary Kimble

My first high-heeled shoes, in the fifties, were spiked three-inch heels, and they were called baby dolls because of the rounded toe. Although it was extremely difficult to walk in them, I knew I had to try, as it was a rite of passage into adulthood.

—Eileen Fond

T-strap shoes (flats) were *the* most fashionable thing a twelve to fifteen-year-old could possibly wear. With nylons of course. Common in black but divine in red.

—Nancy Kinney

One of the great losses of my youth, circa 1959, was that my arch was too high to get a T-strap buckled over it.

—M. Miller

Capezios were the only shoes to wear—so thin and hardly coming up over the sides of your feet.

—Peggy Byrnes

We called them cocktail dresses, but we hardly drank.

—Anna Lee Fuchs

We bought pastel flats at Leeds for $2.98 to $3.98 in the fifties in junior high. Rich girls bought them at Chandlers for a dollar or so more. We only wore them one day a week with those great nylons with the seams. It wasn't the school that was limiting us to one day a week but some sort of informal consensus by our parents. I don't know if they were worried that they would "ruin our feet" or that they looked too grown-up.

—Regina Neuman

I grew up in the San Fernando Valley, where shorts (we didn't call them short shorts then, although they were just as abbreviated) seemed like formal attire. I recall my mother and other neighborhood women watering the lawn wearing shorts, halter tops, and turbans over their pin curls. When rubber thongs—we called them flip-flops—came into fashion, this was big news. Husbands and fathers didn't like them. Believe it or not, the big issue was noise: the sound of the rubber flip-flopping against the bottoms of your rock-hard (from going barefoot) feet. If you could walk quietly in them, then you could wear them—that was the rule. I recall how much more comfortable it became to run out on the hot asphalt street to buy a Big Stick Popsicle wearing flip-flops. Once you got over the soreness between your big and second toe, they were like a second skin.

—Rochelle Reed

My eighth-grade homeroom teacher demanded that all the girls wear socks to school. She even went so far as to have a sock check every morning. If you weren't wearing socks, you got a demerit, and I thought that would be the worst thing in the world to happen to me. Anyway, I desperately wanted to wear flats with no socks. Capezio flats with Peds were the rage. I took a chance and wore flats with Peds, but I brought one sock with me to school. When the teacher made her routine sock check, I had one socked foot dangling in the aisle and the other sockless foot carefully folded under me, hidden under my dress. My adrenaline was flowing, but she passed me by without a word.

—Christine Robinson

My shoe fetish began with buying my first pair of Margaret Jerrold shoes on sale for $9 when I was nine years old. They were half price and I was in heaven. My mother shouted that I had no right to spend that kind of money on a pair of shoes even if they were on sale. Seven dollars should have been the maximum.

—Barbara Diamond

Remember see-through plastic shoes, belts, and purses? Fifteen minutes after being put on, the shoes and belt were no longer transparent but were opaque with perspiration. I suppose the shoes were meant to be reminiscent of Cinderella's glass slipper but then Cinderella probably didn't sweat. The plastic purse was greatly impractical because (1) most of them had sharp corners to inflict pain on oneself or one's escort, and (2) everyone could see exactly what the contents of the purse were.

—Carolyn Zucker

Even without the poodle, we'd know this is a picture from the fifties. The clues: the gloves, the stole (one side in the same fabric as the dress—very chic in those days), and the plastic purse (this style also came in clear plastic, and a colorful, coordinated-to-the-dress-of-the-day scarf was artfully draped inside to conceal the rest of the contents). (Judy Lamm)

We carried plastic box purses. They cost $3.98 and came in a variety of colors. When you forgot to close the little latch firmly, everything spilled on the ground with a loud crash.

—*Regina Neuman*

Sometime in elementary school, we discovered suitcase purses. These were plastic and about the size of a shoebox, with a lock and key. At that age there wasn't really much to keep inside, so we really had to look around for something worth keeping under lock and key. Mine was gray. We couldn't carry them comfortably, but we had to have them. We put them on our desks. That was unacceptable to our teacher, and we were all sent to the principal's office, the only time I ever went.

—*Lyn Messner*

I went to high school in Alabama for two years. There was only one acceptable purse style: the bucket. It was a rigid oval with flaps over the top. Black or brown in winter, white in summer. If you knew what was good for you, you carried that purse. If you didn't, you were branded as an oddball. Reputations were made or broken by that stupid bucket purse.

—*Ellen Ekman*

Bucket bags were often the first real handbag style owned by an adolescent girl. When I was growing up in Maine, you had to have one or you were as good as dead.

—*Nancy Kinney*

I had quite a wardrobe of gloves from short white to long black. At dances, some girls smoked in their long white gloves and got nicotine stains on the fingers. I think they were supposed to slip their hands out through the slits at the wrist and tuck them [the gloves] up inside before lighting up.

—*Rose Mary Kimble*

Recollections from junior and senior high schools are of competitive dressing, or "How I managed to dress like the rich girls." The summer uniform was Lanz dresses. The winter was minklam (a fuzzy wool-and-nylon-and-angora blend) sweaters, and straight skirts in wool with a kick pleat in the back. The skirt color had to match the sweater perfectly. Then, of course, you only needed a collection of print scarves, folded in a triangle around your neck.

My mother, the seamstress, was the master strategist in the dressing game. We would trek to downtown Los Angeles, where we bought the *actual* Lanz fabrics and the wool dyed to match the minklam. Even the heart-shaped buttons. My mother would copy a Lanz down to the exact rickrack.

—*Gloria Casvin*

A single circle pin meant you were not going steady with anyone; a double circle meant you were.

—*Beth Padon*

Circle pins evoke a real negative feeling. I don't know why. I didn't like them then, and now they still seem ridiculous and sterile.

—*Peggy Byrnes*

I did have a circle pin, but had to wear it on the sly because supposedly, wearing one meant you were a virgin and my straight-laced mother said that wasn't the kind of thing nice girls talked about or insinuated. Also, ankle braclets meant you were loose.

—*Michele Burgess*

Ankle bracelets were worn only by the bad girls.

—*Pat Mathis*

We had sweater clasps: two fancy alligator clips connected by a chain or string of pearls. We wore them to hold our sweaters over our shoulder without putting our arms in the sleeves.

—*Michele Burgess*

The only belt I really remember was called a cinch belt, popular in Milwaukee around 1953–1954. It was rather wide, three to four inches of elastic that snapped together in front. The snaps were decorated and the elastic came in many colors, also in stripes. They worked out best if you were thin. If you were heavy the elastic tended to roll from the top and bottom.

—*Sandy Whitehurst*

I would wear wide belts pulled so tight that I could hardly breathe. But having a twenty-inch waist, or the appearance of it, was much more important than breathing.

—*Ellen Ekman*

My favorite belt as a teenager was a very wide (3½ inches), red stretch cinch. I wore this with both full and pencil-slim, tight skirts.

—*Carolyn Zucker*

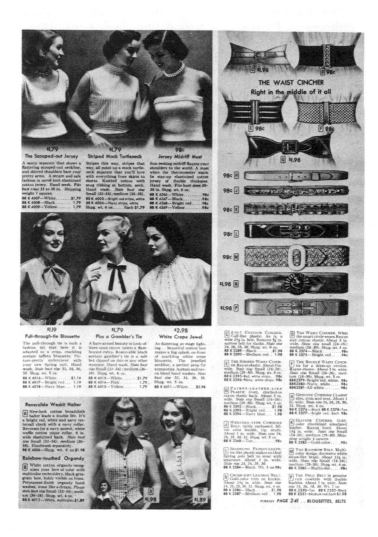

Waist cinchers were the *belt in the fifties. The best ones were three-inch-wide elastic; they fit snugly but permitted some breathing (not all belts did).* (Sears, Roebuck and Company)

Pop-it beads were my favorite costume jewelry in the fourth and fifth grades. I would fool around with them all day, mixing the colors to match my summer shorts and tops.

—Marilyn Overholt

The best thing about pop-it beads was that jewelry became a great toy.

—Sara B. Chase

Pop beads were some psychologists' subtle way of teaching eye-hand coordination.

—Linda Dahl

Most of us peroxided our bangs at least once. The brunettes' hair turned orange. The blondes were not so obvious. Our peroxide came directly from our chemistry lab.

—Anna Lee Fuchs

My mother's tips and quips:

- Angora sweaters make men sneeze.
- Ankle bracelets, high heels and slacks, and pierced ears are tacky.
- Perfume, though seductive, goes home with a man.
- Pre-dirty your saddle shoes to be cool.
- Pantyhose are a deterrent to men.
- Wedgies are an insult to pretty feet.
- Platforms are for whores.
- Flat shoes rob your sexuality.
- Culottes make you look like you can't make up your mind.
- Men's shirts are great if that's all you wear (in private).

—Anne Wehrer

In the fifties little scarves were tied at the neck, worn with sweater sets and blouses. They were frequently paired with two scatter pins. For some reason you always got both for Christmas. Kerchiefs were called babushkas. Also running neck and neck with babushkas was a little dressier headgear. We just called them scarves—maybe five feet long, eight to ten inches wide, with fringe on the ends. You folded it in half lengthwise, put it over your head, tied it under your

Shawls, stoles, and shrugs were practical summer cover-ups in the fifties. Shawls and stoles were somewhat attractive; shrugs, never. The lower left picture shows silk scarves for as little as 98 cents! It also shows the old-world way most women wore them. The neck scarf (K) came in fifties colors of pink, white, and black. (Sears, Roebuck and Company)

chin, and then threw one end over your left shoulder and the other over your right. They were generally beautiful plaids, the better ones being of lightweight wool.

—Sandy Whitehurst

I was a midwestern girl growing up in Detroit and it was a big deal to go to New York City. We would go to the museums and art galleries and to Greenwich Village. There was a drugstore there, on the corner of Fifth Avenue and Eighth Street, that had great shades of lipstick. Pale pinks and white. This was the fifties and way before Revlon or any of the biggies had those colors. I'd buy them and Fred Braun shoes. When I got back to Detroit, I'd always drop the name: "These are Fred Braun shoes." They were handmade, hand-stitched, harness leather sandals. Very bohemian. In those days I thought anything from New York was great.

—Gloria List

Even through high school, my mother would periodically throw open my closet door and scrutinize my wardrobe. She felt I was always wearing the same few outfits. True. She'd spy something I hadn't worn in months, probably because I hated it. She'd grab it and say in her best Captain Queeg imitation, "You haven't worn *this* in a long time. You'll wear it tomorrow." It meant you'll-do-what-I-say-as-long-as-I'm-paying-the-bills-around-here. I would wear whatever it was, but it usually ruined my day.

—Ellen Ekman

For girls growing up in a small town, a trip to the big city to shop for school clothes in late August was the thrill of back-to-school. The *smell* of the big-city department stores is still memorable, and can be reexperienced by inhaling new things one buys even today. Intoxication! Even though the smell may be the "finish" or sizing on new clothes. Each year, one would wonder if girls' sizes or junior sizes would be the order of the day. Occasionally a Misses size blouse could be purchased, if it was made in size 30. The best blouses came in size 30.

—Nancy Kinney

Initials on everything in the fifties! Dickeys, friendship rings, ankle bracelets, slips, sweaters, shoulder bags, pencil cases. One never forgot who one was.

—*Janice Morgan*

Some of my friends wore colored-rim glasses with winged corners—to go with their doe eyes, to look like Audrey Hepburn, which nobody ever did.

—*Anna Lee Fuchs*

I had a shaggy haircut just like Audrey Hepburn's. People would say, "Oh, you look just like Audrey Hepburn." Sure. But I did have sort of a gamin look, a little undernourished. I wore black tights and ballet slippers like she did in *Funny Face*. Before that, only old ladies in Europe and nuns wore black stockings.

—*Gloria List*

Everybody dressed so sloppy in high school that the school started "dress-up day." I think it was Fridays and you had to wear heels, etc. We all did it happily. In fact, it didn't matter what we wore; it was fun so long as *everyone* wore it. There was no room for eccentrics.

—*Peggy Byrnes*

What I can remember most about my high school friends is that we all dressed alike. It identified us as a group. To every athletic event we wore our white blouses, school sweaters, jeans (rolled up), white socks, and saddle shoes. There was always a space of leg showing between the jeans and the socks.

—*Anna Lee Fuchs*

Bonnie Doon socks, the same color as the outfit you were wearing, were the big look in San Francisco in 1958–1959. I had an emerald-green wool skirt, dyed-to-match cardigan sweater, and I wore Bonnie Doons in the exact same color! They had to be rolled down to the ankle so that each one looked like a doughnut.

—*M. Miller*

I remember being ridiculed for wearing Bermuda shorts. Tomboy friends and I were together at the Carvel ice cream stand in Massapequa. One of the girls from a "sexier" clique made some terrible comment on our weird shorts, probably that they were butch or something. We read *Seventeen* religiously and probably bought them because they were in the magazine. But I remember that the girl who made the remark was wearing them a few months later.

—Peggy Byrnes

I went to the High School of Music and Art (sort of like *Fame* only much more academic). We all began the black tights-black leotards craze. We were the original hippie children. Black clothing was in—black tights, especially with skirts worn over them, and pale faces with dark eyes.

—Laurie Burrows Grad

The first time I wore stockings, I was ten years old. It seems ridiculous now when I look at little ten-year-old girls and imagine them in such a getup. My girl friend Judy and I celebrated our birthdays together: We took the train into New York City with our mothers and went to lunch and the movies. We wanted to be very grown-up that day. I was conscious of the stockings every second. Although they were really anchored quite securely to the garter, I was panicked that they would fall down. We had to stop at Woolworth's after lunch so I could get these rubber garters that I surreptitiously rolled up each leg right there in the aisle while my mother and Judy's mother shielded me from prying eyes. I'm surprised they didn't give me gangrene. Even with them I wasn't relaxed. I hated stockings. I hated being grown-up. Maybe I didn't want to grow up after all. When I got home I took the whole stinking getup off and shoved it back in my dresser and refused even to consider stockings for months. I was only goaded into them again when Judy showed up at school in a pair.

—Ellen Ekman

My Garboesque mother with the Grable legs tried to instill feminine grace and dignity in her twelve-year-old tomboy, who preferred sailing boats and climbing trees to designer Easter suits complete with gloves, hat, corsage, and stockings. Stockings were about growing up (like lipstick), a puberty ritual of womanhood. Her instructions for putting on stockings:

- Finger and toenails must be smooth.
- Begin by making a fist and gliding your hand through the stocking.
- Turn it inside out.
- Put your hand back through the stocking to grasp the toe with your other hand.
- Hold the heel and pull the toe through, making it easy to slip your foot inside.
- Gently place the seam between your thumb and index finger.
- Now slowly guide the seam up the center of your leg from heel to thigh.
- Carefully fold the top of the stocking over a flat garter to a point just about your knee.
- Repeat with second stocking.
- Remember: If you don't get it right, you'll only be uncomfortable once—all day!

Mastering the correct positioning of a garter belt to assure straight seams came after I was more at home with my newfound body. I still wear seamed stockings because the men in my life (and I) get off on them. They are complimentary, provocative, and a bit naughty.

—Anne Wehrer

The seams were always crooked. I knew a few girls who tried to get away without wearing hose to school by using eye makeup to create a seam on the backs of their legs. Most got caught. Seams don't smear.

—Sandy Whitehurst

Garter belts were the greatest joke ever concocted by man for woman to wear. I remember the scars from the fasteners engraved on my legs from junior high on. Just to look pretty in hose. What torture!

—Marilyn Overholt

I hated garter belts and seamed stockings. Always being somewhat of a dorky kid, my seams were perpetually zigzagging in the vicinity

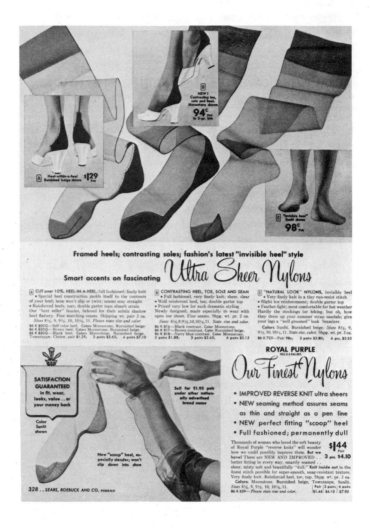

Even though seamless nylons were available in the early fifties, women preferred seamed stockings with sandals. The center pair shown here, with contrasting heel, toe, sole, and seam, was billed as "made especially to wear with open toe shoes." (Sears, Roebuck and Company)

of the back of my legs, and I always had two little round dents in the back of my thighs from sitting on those stinking garters.

—*Michele Burgess*

There was always a problem of some sort with garter belts and stockings. Usually the stockings were too long and had to be adjusted, over and over, up into the garter. If you ran out of brown top and had to hook it into the stocking proper, the stockings ran. Sometimes the garter elastic would get stretched and *that* required more adjusting. We were forever ducking into ladies' rooms to fix our stockings.

—*Rose Mary Kimble*

When I got my first garter belt, I wore it alone, without stockings, to "get used to it." I didn't go far, just out to mail a letter or something like that. But horror of horrors, my mother told my friend's mother, who told her daughter, who snickered at me in school.

—*M. Miller*

Garter belts were out and panty girdles were in. If you did not need a long-leg panty girdle, you wore one anyway and that was that. Miniskirts began to appear. Some ignorant girls continued to wear panty girdles and old-fashioned stockings with the new shorter skirts. We all know what happened when they sat down or crossed their knees.

At last, pantyhose became affordable. But some girls bought the kind that were reinforced or knit in darker nylon at the thigh so the tops of their stockings *still* showed when [they were] sitting in a miniskirt. Disgusting. Add to this the wearing of reinforced-toe stockings with sandals or open-toe shoes. Beneath contempt. Thank God reinforced-heel stockings were a thing of the past. Otherwise one would have to suffer this fashion abuse as well.

—*Nancy Kinney*

As far back as my college days, I'm sure I was never fashionable. For one thing, I could never afford it and for another, I came from a casual, beach community. I do remember owning seven pairs of sandals and one pair of nylon stockings and going barelegged to class every day. I did have a regulation garter belt and even wore a girdle,

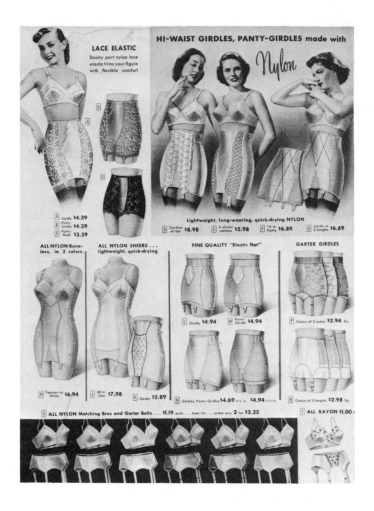

These all-in-ones and long-line girdles, especially the ones with zippers, look more medieval than mid-twentieth century. They were everyday wear thirty years ago. (Sears, Roebuck and Company)

size extra small, that *Seventeen* magazine said was necessity. I think I wore the girdle a couple of times in discomfort before giving it to the Goodwill. I wonder if anyone ever bought it.

—*Dawn Sturgill*

I attended a parochial high school in the mid-fifties, and part of our uniform was hose. Pantyhose hadn't really made it yet, so garter belts were it for most of my friends. I wore a marvelous lightweight stretch panty that had detachable garters called Suspants. They were the best for that time. You still had little bumps on your thighs from the four garters, but you were spared all the ridges on your hips and backside from the belt. God, I love pantyhose. (Please note that I wore this in Milwaukee with dresses in zero weather, and that space between the panty and the top of the stocking got cold.)

—*Sandy Whitehurst*

All those slips and garter belts, etc., seemed simple, not tedious at all. It's amazing, because I was a tomboy.

—*Peggy Byrnes*

When I first started wearing hose—1952 or so—I had the hideous struggle with garter belts and seams—just like Mother. As I got heavier, I welcomed those torturous girdles with the hose clips in them, as they seemed to enable one to fit more smoothly into sheath skirts. When panty hose finally came out, I was in my early years of my first job out of college, much slimmer and vastly relieved to have pull-on hose. Was it pantyhose that made miniskirts possible?

—*Sara B. Chase*

In the summer, we always wore a slip so no one could see through our skirts no matter how hot it was.

—*Anna Lee Fuchs*

Full slips were pretty and warm in winter. My straps always seemed to fall down. It seemed that most bras in the fifties were not very attractive, so if you were in something sheer, the slip was great. But always *with* a bra.

—*Sandy Whitehurst*

In high school I remember receiving a gift of underwear. There were seven pairs of panties, each with the name of a day of the week. I would be so upset if the Monday pair wasn't clean and I had to wear Friday's underwear on Monday.

—Anna Lee Fuchs

Conjuring up the ideal figure of spaghetti-strap, strapless, and tight sheath dresses was quite an endeavor. Reorganization of the body was necessary and began with the many-boned Merry Widow to hold the midriff in and push up the bosom. To keep tummy and thighs from bulging, the elasticized girdle extended from the waist to approximately five inches above the knees. These shackles probably held off the sexual revolution for a few years.

—Carolyn Zucker

I loved wearing spaghetti-strap dresses but hated the fact that I would have to wear a strapless bra underneath, as those old strapless bras had stays in them that would stick into my flesh and leave marks for hours after taking them off.

—Eileen Fond

I was a late bloomer and have been slender (or, some would say, "gaunt") all my life. My sister, my cousin, and I all had the same physique, and during our high school days we were very conscious of the fact that our figures did not live up to the expectations Hollywood had for us. My cousin, who was adventurous, devised a remedy which she called her "surprise." It was very simple really. She stuffed scarves into her bra until she had a more "feminine" outline. We were delighted and figured that if it ever got to the point that a boy discovered the stuffing, we would yell, "Surprise!" I later refined the system by cutting up nylon stockings into small pieces. Much later, I realized it was easier just to buy a padded bra, but we were too shy in those days.

—Dawn Sturgill

Circular-stitched cotton bras wadded up after a jillion washings and looked real gross under sweaters. Any girl with any sense stopped buying them and switched to other styles. Maidenform was a real offender in this regard.

—Nancy Kinney

Merry Widows were de rigueur *under all those fussy tulle formals. These symbols of womanhood had their price: They were iron corsets, hampering movement, breathing, and eating. But we'd give all that up for a twenty-two-inch waist.* (Sears, Roebuck and Company)

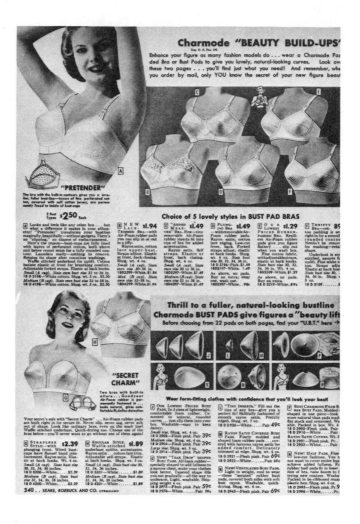

In addition to heavily padded bras with coy names like "Pretender" and "Secret Charm," Sears offered twenty-two types of bust pads, aka falsies. Here's just part of the falsie line: round or teardrop, just nipples, full pads with sculptured nipples, nippleless, and ventilated. (Sears, Roebuck and Company)

Bras were cotton, stitched in concentric circles, which made one appear, under those nice short-sleeved pullover sweaters, to have perpetually erect nipples. Maybe that's why all the "nice girls" wore sweater sets—a double layer to camouflage.

—Sara B. Chase

We wore bathing suits (often strapless) with little boy legs or a little skirt in front to cover up the crotch or the fact that we had one.

—Anna Lee Fuchs

Clothes before the chemise were very fitted, so this was a new freedom. They tended to be somewhat like the dresses of the twenties but a bit longer—below the knee. Boys didn't like them.

—Sandy Whitehurst

I believe the chemise dress was one of the ugliest styles foisted upon American women by designers. The dress disregarded the bustline and the waist, dropping straight down until it fit tightly over the buttocks. My chemise was yellow, and I looked like a waddling stick of butter.

—Carolyn Zucker

Sometime around my college years, the chemise dress was in. I remember my father asking why I would hide my waist (which was pretty good) and show off my hips (which weren't so good). I think that was the first time I really considered that it might be better to look good rather than fashionable.

—Gloria Casvin

I think the willingness to try anything ended for me with the sack dress. Was it 1958? It was thin red cotton, and I wore it once and tried to forget it.

—Peggy Byrnes

In order to really show the tent dress as a "tent," it needed to show its shape, hence a little heavier, stiffer fabric. Not too exciting to people with skinny legs who looked like bells walking around in them.

—Sandy Whitehurst

Bathing suits in the early fifties were nothing if not modest. No hint of exposed bosom, no hint of exposed hip. Torsos were encased, boned, wired, girdled, and shirred. (Sears, Roebuck and Company)

I had a chemise I still love to think about. White ribbed piqué with a sailor collar and red-and-white-striped knit trim (neckerchief and snap-in dickey in the V-neck). I'd seen it at Joseph Magnin and wanted it for Easter, but Mom said it was too expensive, $25 in 1959. Happily, Dad thought his little girl deserved the best, so he drove me back down to buy it. When it bit the dust, I cut off the buttons, which I still have—gold with an eagle emblem.

—M. Miller

Here's what I never wore: a Pendleton skirt.

I had a friend in high school who had not one but twenty-one Pendleton skirts. I loved them. I coveted them. I was miserable that I had a friend with straight posture, clear skin, perfect breasts, *and* twenty-one Pendleton skirts. The skirts were plaid and pleated, but most important, they were reversible. The pleats were sewn together from the waist to hip and then flared to the knee, so that a green-and-blue plaid skirt looked predominantly green on one side and predominantly blue when reversed.

It's not true that I never wore one. When I went off to college, I bought one. I went off to college with my new Pendleton skirt and my old friend, who by this time had moved into Chanel suits and thought that Pendleton skirts were for immature teenagers. My first year in college I gained thirty pounds, and whenever I put on my Pendleton skirt, I looked like Queen Elizabeth.

Here's what I honestly never wore: a Chanel suit.

—Nora Ephron

The Sixties

For clothing, the sixties was a decade of the sacred and the profane. In the early years, we were so mesmerized by the refined tastes of Jackie Kennedy that we dressed like carbon copies. Toward the end of the decade, we were infatuated with the wild and irreverent anti-clothes of the hippies. We would wear anything, including nothing. To go from pillboxes and pearls to tie-dye undershirts in a few short years reflects the radical changes that were taking place in our society as a whole. We were searching, sorting out, shedding "the shackles of our minds." As always, our dress mirrored everything that was going on inside our heads.

Jackie Kennedy, from the vantage point of twenty years later, may seem like just a simple, conservative dresser, hardly a trend-setter. But her influence was so far-reaching that even today, it has blinded us to how new, how well thought out her style was. Her example affected us all—from socialities to sorority girls to suburban housewives.

Before JFK moved into the White House, women dressed a lot like, well, Pat Nixon. Maybe we would have continued that look of fussy, undefined prints if the election had gone the other way. The "more is more" look.

Once Jackie became First Lady, the paring down began. We didn't need collars all the time, or long sleeves. Prints suddenly seemed unnecessarily cluttered alongside a pure, well-chosen solid.

We wanted just the essentials, please. Moderation. To look like ladies. And the First Lady led the way. The classic Jackie ensemble was a two-piece dress or suit with a semifitted top ending just below the waist, at the top of the hipbone. An overblouse, yes, but never blousy. Often there was no collar at all, just a simple round or oval neckline. Sleeves ranged from sleeveless to three-quarter length. Not full length. Just below the elbow would do, even in winter. Skirts were slim A-lines, midknee or just below the knee. Pumps were low-heeled, conservative, and comfortable. Fashion devotees knew that low-slung pumps were essential to the look, but less-aware Jackie clones stuck with high-heeled spikes. Some suits were double-breasted, Chanel-like (but always made in America) bouclés with contrasting lapels. Evening dresses were Empire style (and if we listened intently, we heard it pronounced "om-peer" not "em-pyre").

Jackie's style didn't change perceptibly when she was forced to switch from French designers to American ones after the election year brouhaha over her expensive foreign tastes. It wasn't the look that people objected to. It was, why weren't American clothes good enough for our own First Lady? So Oleg Cassini replaced Givenchy without missing a beat. Once we started copying her look, suddenly we were Francophiles too. After all, we knew enough to pronounce it "om-peer."

Jackie had unbelievable clarity in her dress. She understood cut, color, and the art of pulling it all together into a total package. Her detractors (surely, we sniffed, they were politically motivated) cried out that any woman could look that good if she spent the time and money on it that the First Lady did. Sure, with her dough, we could copy rather nicely, but we could never have originated it.

Big buttons—huge ones, two inches in diameter—were a Jackie trademark. One (two at the most) to close a jacket. And that button was near the neck, not the waist. It was a minor but revolutionary concept.

Jackie's pillbox was the last of the serious hats. It was perky, simple, and chic. But once the pillbox ran its course, hats would be relegated almost exclusively to eccentrics and attention seekers.

Because the pillbox and the clean neckline focused attention on the head, the hairdo took on new importance. The style, as Jackie wore it, was rounded and lifted from the scalp a moderate amount. But the bouffant, when adapted in the provinces by women and hairdressers with less sense of proportion than Jackie and her Kenneth, took on the dimensions of an inflated balloon. They started adding a guiche curl (murdering the word, calling it "geech") over each cheek. To keep each curled in a perfect C, we taped it to our cheeks at night or applied clear nail polish to maintain its perfect shape.

Jackie made simplicity a religion. When she left the White House and was "permitted" a less rigidly prescribed life-style, she taught us that even T-shirts and slacks could be chic. Eventually we turned away from the Jackie look. Maybe we didn't see enough of her after the assassination to keep a clear image of her style in our heads. Maybe it was just too much of a good thing—or too much of the same thing. It was a rather limited style: one silhouette, strictly solid colors, safe, sane, tasteful. There was a sameness, a flatness, a nonevolving quality to it. We ultimately rejected this dignified, ladylike appearance to dress like Lolitas.

Audrey Hepburn looked more like Jackie's twin in the sixties than the poor but elegant gamin we had known in the fifties. After all, she was a real woman now—a real, rich woman. And she obviously spent money on clothes. Her taste and Jackie's seemed to coincide. For a while they were twin goddesses, high priestesses of the one-button–pillbox faith.

The Jackie look was not inaugurated on the stroke of midnight January 1, 1960. Some of us didn't catch on till '61 or '62. And even then, Jackie's suits and pillboxes were more knock-'em-dead outfits for rush week and country club luncheons than knock-around clothes for day to day. We wore sporty fifties styles well into the next decade.

Brigitte Bardot, a woman as different from Jackie and Audrey as could be imagined, was a bigger fashion influence in the sixties than we recall. We are too busy joking about how good she looked in a towel or *au naturel* to remember that she was a stylesetter. With her dress, her hairdo, her makeup, she taught us how to look

Audrey Hepburn at her Jackie Kennedy-est: pillbox, three-quarter sleeve, three-button, semifitted suit, gloves (don't they look wrinkled and ridiculous to us now?), and a chain purse. Very elegant, very expensive. (Universal Pictures Company)

cheap, in the sense that our mothers meant when they disapproved of what we wore. Too floozy-like, too flashy, too immodest. The sixties were a cheap decade. Not even Jackie could save us from our penchant for tackiness.

Bardot's 1959 wedding dress, pink gingham with white lace trim, caught the world's attention, and by 1960, gingham and lace (accessorized by a tiny triangular kerchief) were summer wardrobe essentials all over America. Gingham could be saucy as well as sweet. It was called the St.-Tropez look, and it was only the first wave. Over the years there would be several invasions from the French Riviera. Bardot led the attack. The second wave followed in

The pink gingham dress, left, was a knock-off of Brigitte Bardot's 1959 wedding dress. Hers had a scoop neck (but not as scooped as you'd imagine), but otherwise they are the same style. Gingham became a best-seller, seen in a new sex-kitten light, before the honeymoon was over. (Sears, Roebuck and Company)

1961: bell bottoms and high crop tops with a very bare midriff between. Youthful, cocky, bell bottoms were a big breakthrough in the static pants styles of the fifties.

The French Riviera vied with California for fashion attention. It was the battle of the beaches. Both wanted to be credited with giving birth to the new styles—the bikini and bell bottoms. Both were youth crazy, and they copied from each other.

Jax pants were the California capri look. The height of Jax-ness was a pair of gingham capris worn with flat Capezio thong sandals. Both the capris and the Capezios came in scads of bright, sunny colors. Jax capris were lined. Gingham alone would have been too flimsy, impossible to fit snugly, and Jax fit with perhaps a half inch to spare. The classic Jax capri had no waistband, just a finishing band turned back on the hip. It was impossible to wear a belt with them, or keep a blouse tucked inside. (We turned to crop tops as the best solution.) Like all fashionable pants then, they ended above the anklebone. It wasn't until the late sixties that we adopted a longer pants leg.

A new method for making flat knits (heavy enough to hold their shape for sheaths and suits as well as pants) made big news in 1960. Knits were no longer strictly for flowing jerseys and Italian striped tops. These new knits made fitting easy. The semifitted Jackie look was simpler to achieve, simpler to sew. Knits quickly took over the pants industry. Stretch pants, often in a nylon called Helanca, with a stirrup strap under the instep were new in the stores in 1961. The stirrup kept the pants from creeping up the leg. We wanted our pants to fit skintight, and without that strap they would have crept upward into every crevice possible. The strap gave us sleekness. Stretch pants were so tight we didn't need girdles underneath, rather a heady experience. But the pants were every bit as confining as girdles. For the most part, we made no attempt to hide the strap. It was visible with flats. After a few years, we coordinated the stretch pants with ankle-high boots, giving a much smoother line. The boots were really the first fashion boots to come along. Before then, they had been seen as utilitarian only, as mere galoshes.

Crop tops were eminently practical. We didn't have to worry about a blouse bunching up or coming untucked, or keeping a belt at waist level in the back when we bent over. Nobody could really see up them. Capris always zipped in the back. Fly fronts were for men back then. Our idea of a well-cut pair of black flats was one that showed toe cleavage. (Columbia Pictures Corporation)

Shifts, simple waistless dresses, were big in the summer of 1963. They were often as ungainly as the late, unlamented sack, with gathers that started and ended in disadvantageous spots. The best were plain body skimmers with no gathers. Instead of wearing them to the office with pumps and pearls, we wore them to the beach, the market, and summer school. We found that it was easy to hang around in a shift; it was as cool as pedal pushers, almost as cool as shorts. Marimekkos were the best. If you could sew, you could make a shift out of a yard of fabric.

Plain white sneakers took over from saddle shoes as the preferred school shoe. The sneakers had to be pure and plain, with no fancy stitching, soles, or colors. There were two ways to keep white sneakers white: shoe polish and the washing machine. Only a nerd put polish on sneakers. We knew enough to throw them in with the rest of the wash. We wore them with socks for a long-legged, all-in-one majorette look. But increasingly we liked sneakers with stockings. The stockings were usually a shade or two darker than skin tone and looked swarthy against the white of the sneakers. Stockings and sneakers were never the height of fashion. They never made *Vogue* or *Women's Wear Daily*, but that's what everyone wore with shirtwaists and with skirts and Garland sweaters.

Early sixties coats gave us several options. Polo coats were still in style as well as shawl-collared cashmeres for dressy occasions. Fur collars were wonderful. The Jackie look called for an Empire or princess-line coat. Car coats were in; toppers were out. We finally gave up the notion that brocade dusters were elegant.

Junior styles were a new concept. The same baby boomers that brought about the subteen and teen fashions of the fifties were responsible for this attention to young women as a separate fashion entity from their mothers. We didn't move from teenagers to matrons on our eighteenth birthdays. And we weren't all five foot six. We had money to spend, so manufacturers were there to serve us. Perhaps we would forget about wearing safe and serviceable black dresses after all. Perhaps we'd like something "fun." It was a whole new concept: fun. Fun clothes were something your mother would never wear. The St.-Tropez look was fun. Our mothers wouldn't wear hip-huggers or minis.

Mary Quant had opened the first boutique in the Chelsea section of London in 1955. She called the shop Bazaar. It would take a few years for her revolutionary design and vision to catch on in America. Her reputation for kookiness evolved slowly, and her styles moved, step by step, farther away from the old way of dressing. In 1960, Quant created knee-length jumpers in a silhouette that was called "the look of the precocious child." It was a radical change from the older-is-better notion that we were accustomed to. By 1962, the Mary Quant look was going full tilt, with checkerboard dresses that were sparse, figure-skimming, and short. We felt the first tremors of the youthquake. Quant put on fashion shows with high-spirited, prancing girl models scampering down the runway, not the remote, carefully paced mannequins of the fifties. She was opening us up to the fashion-is-fun, life-as-theater way of living. Her message was: You'll see the world differently from inside a mod minidress than in a shirtwaist and girdle. She was right. And her timing was perfect.

Mary Quant was her own best model. We were always on the lookout for a new gamin idol in our lives. Quant was perky. She kicked up her heels and played pranks on friends. Her dark hair was short, straight, and blunt-cut. She was as much fun as her clothes were.

In short shifts and jumpers, we looked like Mary Quant dolls. In rejecting the matronly look that automatically added ten years to the age of the wearer, the Quant look oscillated the other way. Twenty-year-olds no longer looked thirty; they now looked ten. But to set everyone straight that we were really women of the world, we sent out a clue. Eyes—we blackened them to the point of ghoulishness with shadow, liner, and mascara. The graveyard look was high fashion. We were convinced that we could never be seen in public without eyeliner. Before breakfast, harsh black lines were drawn across each lid.

We focused on eyes but neglected lips. No more Fire and Ice, no more Cherries in the Snow. We wanted just the ice, just the snow. We wore white lipstick or the palest pink. We thought the blacker the eye, the paler the lip, the more stunning the face. The dark eyes and white lips of the harlot contrasted with the pink gingham minidress. We had two totally opposite notions going, the classic saint and sinner, the whore with the heart of gold. In a way, they balanced each other. Not *too* sweet, not *too* sexy. But in trying to achieve a balance between little girl and world-class sophisticate, we kept moving back on the seesaw. A little shorter skirt, a little more eye makeup. Pictures of those styles are most embarrassing today. We had gone too far. Fully extended, the mod look mixed pristine white lacey tights and Mary Janes and sappy pastel microminis with the gates-of-hell makeup of *The Three Penny Opera*.

Although they looked the opposite, these clothes were liberating, feminist. We were being overtly sexy yet able to maintain control. It was an important but awkward growth stage. Before the mini-mod look, we dressed in feminine styles. We were mothers, wives, and daughters in our shirtwaists, mere dates in our sheaths. We couldn't reveal too much cleavage, too much leg, or surely we would be ravished. We weren't certain men could handle such a tease as an inch of thigh. We had given up the concept of the chaperone, so our clothes would have to help us keep order. We could dress somewhat alluringly for dates. A man should think that in a moment of passion he could just rip the strapless gown from our bodies to find our supple flesh beneath (when he'd really find a formidable Merry Widow). But the strapless gown couldn't be so daring that he'd actually do it. Our clothes were meant to heighten the fantasy yet keep us from being attacked.

Minis changed all that. They were so sexy that we could never have worn them in public without thinking, "I can handle it." Psychological armor was a fashion accessory. We could not feel like putty in men's hands. They had to be putty in ours. We could say no, beat it, get lost or . . . you, I like. We didn't have to wait to be noticed. We dressed so we would always be noticed and then *we* would accept or reject the attention as we chose. To wear a mini was to work from a position of strength. It still made us sex objects, but we were sex objects with a sense of our own power. Although

Ladylike perfection, 1967. This is a look we were all after. Mia Farrow wears a Jackie/Courrèges mini (just qualifying for mini status at the top of the knee), low, square-heeled pumps, and a quilted Chanel-type bag with gloves. (Paramount Pictures Corporation)

the mini appeared to be a step backward for women's liberation, it was a breakthrough.

By the time *Life* proclaimed, "Here Come the Beatles" in January 1964, the mod look was in full swing here. The British influence was felt everywhere. Jean Shrimpton and Twiggy had The Look, lanky and not a little bit vacuous.

Clothes were graphic in every sense. The contrast of lots of black and white made a strong visual statement. The op art show at the Museum of Modern Art set off fabric copies of Vasarely-inspired checkerboard optics. Pop art gave us Warholesque soup-can shifts. We liked strong prints. Puccis. Dots and strips together were called the Carnaby look and were done up in mini-shirtwaists (with straight skirts, not full ones) and wide clown ties. Mod never stood for moderation. Excess was prized. When harsh colors became a bit of a bore, we switched to pastels, piqué, and gingham, but always short.

The Ivy-League-look manufacturers were thrown into a bankruptcy-threatening state. They chopped off skirts and peddled mini-shirtwaists, mini-cord skirts (to be worn with oxford-cloth shirts, of course). They survived. The Ivy Leaguers couldn't give themselves over completely to the mod look. They could, and did, take up their hems and wait till the threat passed.

Mary Quant drew so much attention with her designs and her madcap escapades that we assume that the mother of the miniskirt was the only designer responsible for the new short look. Not true. At the same time, working in Paris, André Courrèges, a protégé of Balenciaga's, introduced his own minidress look to an entirely different audience. It was the most striking change in couture fashion since the New York of 1947. Courrèges was the first couturier to approach the mini with confidence and authority. His first collection was too extreme for most women, but it was eminently adaptable and refinable. To achieve his rigidly straight lines, Courrèges cut heavy fabrics into figure-skimming minis and tunic-and-pants ensembles. Everything was white, including his two key acccessories, the helmet and the boots. The futuristic total look reflected the new space age. The helmets were silly and made the models look like Parisian space cadets, but Courrèges's ten-inch-high white boots were better received. Soon white boots were knee high, then thigh high. The higher, the better; the whiter, the better. The ultimate groovy look was a micromini and white boots. We felt so young, so free that we didn't even bother to put them away after Labor Day. We weren't a bit bothered by the plasticity of it all.

Another sixties designer, Rudi Gernreich, is better remembered for his absurd fashion statements, like the topless bathing suit and the transparent blouse, than for the serious designing he did then and has done since. He pioneered the use of knits and double-knits, working them into lean, flattering silhouettes. His palette was clear

pinks, yellows, black and white. His knits in the early sixties won
him major design awards. But it wasn't until the topless suit in 1964
that his name became well known. His design, actually a high-
waisted, black knit brief with suspenders, was meant as a commen-
tary on where fashion seemed to be heading. Gernreich appeared
almost taken by surprise that the suit was selling—and being worn.
He seemed to pity attention-seeking women who wore them on the
beaches. Didn't they see the joke?

Before the mini, people considered the knee ugly, not just certain ugly knees but all knees. That women would expose such an
unattractive part of their bodies shocked some people more than a
lack of modesty. Designer Norman Norell's response: "There was
a time when women always had to wear long or three-quarter
sleeves because they said their elbows were ugly. They've learned
to live with ugly elbows and don't give them a thought anymore.
There's nothing worse about a knee joint. Women will learn to live
with ugly knees." How comforting. To whip newly exposed knees
into shape, the Elizabeth Arden Salon in New York scheduled
knee exercises and massages. Other salons followed. Dark knee
makeup, newly on the market, could also give the illusion of
thinner knees. Few women bothered with a beauty routine for
their knees. Keeping their eyes black and their hair ratted was
routine enough. Knees did become acceptable. We quickly forgot
their "inherent" ugliness.

Anyway, men preferred to look past the knee to a hunk of
thigh. But if men thought that minis meant they'd be treated to a
veritable parade of bare legs, they were to be at least partially disappointed. When miniskirts first appeared, women were still wearing brown-topped stockings. Garter gap was a nightmare. If we'd
asked men for their advice, they would have suggested we go barelegged. Not on your life! That would have left us too vulnerable.
We either bit the bullet with stockings until pantyhose were per-
fected or we wore tights. The technology of tights was refined before the technology of sheer pantyhose. White, black, purple, and
especially in fishnet and lace, they left only an outline as a daring
gesture. Tights were proper, modest, and efficient, but men seemed

to think they were a cheap trick. Sure, they saw more little white triangles of cotton in a day than they had in a lifetime of shirtwaists, but as often as not the crotch was carefully encased in lace or purple and in all sorts of new slips and bloomer devices. The fantasy was no longer to rip away the strapless gown but to reach up the micromini to find a mere bikini brief. But most men found one, two, three layers of impediment.

Sheer pantyhose were the mighty legacy of the mini. We loved the illusion of the bare leg much more than the bare leg itself. We liked our legs encased in sheer sausage casings. Pantyhose edited legs. They hid the hair, the blotches, the cellulite. Real or imagined flaws were eliminated, and pantyhose permitted us to present a tightened, monotone version of our legs to the world. Pantyhose, compared with stockings and garters, were emancipation. They permitted us not only comfort but the opportunity to dress more extremely with a certain aplomb: in the micromini. We were testing the limits.

While outerwear was at an all-time outrageous peak of impracticality and attention-seeking, underwear was becoming more practical. The exaggerated curves of the fifties, with the female torso pushed, prodded, and cantilevered into submission (all in the name of femininity and modesty), gradually disappeared. We wanted undergarments that were more natural in shape and less unappealing to the eye. After all, there was a much greater likelihood of someone (a man) seeing them. We were not about to let them see an all-in-one.

Bras were less constructed, less padded, and not always stark white. Our bosoms looked less like twin volcanoes. Men still were breast-fixated, but at least they were fixated on a more natural shape.

Synthetic elastic fibers called Lycra and spandex facilitated new designs in all types of lingerie. Three times as powerful as natural rubber, Lycra could make a girdle with real control. By eliminating the need for bones or stays or zippers, it revolutionized girdlemaking. It could be dyed and knitted into fabrics. Panty girdles became almost the universal choice over regular girdles. With a back seam instead of no seam, the panty girdle gave a much more natural silhouette. As girdle legs became longer (and finally finished off with a two-inch cuff of lacy elastic) garter tabs were put up inside the cuff rather than at the bottom. It was a major aesthetic breakthrough. The stocking top, the ugly brown part, went up inside the girdle and made a smooth line. We were in girdle heaven. We couldn't ask for anything more (except not to wear a girdle). We still didn't like the thought of anything showing with our miniskirts, but if something had to show, a two-inch lace border was preferable to a brown top and garter gap.

For years girdle manufacturers had touted them as necessary for every woman from sixteen to the grave. If we bought that line, then we had to wear girdles to hang laundry on the line and go bowling, for hiking and gardening, as well as for work. The ads showed smiling, spirited twenty-year-olds wearing girdles for all these activities. There was official acknowledgment that women were enduring a ridiculous amount of discomfort.

But when the first ads for pantyhose came out in the early sixties, there was a sudden release of secret information. Why, girdle manufacturers had known all along what they were subjecting us to. But until they had the technology to offer us something better, their lips were sealed. One of the first ads for pantyhose badmouthed the girdle-stocking axis as "[they] bump, protrude, dig into your skin. They cause thigh bulge known as garter gap, that skin condition known as garter tattoo . . . antique appliances women use to hold stockings up . . ." We couldn't have said it better ourselves.

Pantyhose, once the shaping and sizing were gotten down pat, were a miracle. They could cover, control, and look natural at the same time. They made the miniskirt phenomenon possible (and vice versa). We could let men see our pantyhose—on and off our bodies. Some women, excessively concerned about jiggling flesh, wore panty girdles over the hose. Manufacturers didn't seem to catch on that women no longer needed garter tabs and didn't eliminate them from girdles until the late seventies.

Even after pantyhose were firmly entrenched in the market and in our hearts, girdle manufacturers were still trying to salvage some business by improving the girdle-stocking combination. In 1969, all sorts of systems were offered by which a now much longer stocking could be attached to a panty brief at hip level by hooks, snaps, and Velcro. They promised a sleek, no-bulge line, but we knew that pantyhose did that best.

Lycra was making all sorts of new underwear possible, like bra slips. Ankle-length pant-liners in spandex were another example of one step forward, two steps back. Flesh-colored body stockings, lightweight all-in-ones, were fabulous and were worn under crochet dresses for optimum effect.

In the sixties underpants went from grown-up white diapers to skimpy printed nylon bikinis. Matched to colored bras, they looked more like beachwear than the garments we had worn a few short years before.

Manufacturers had to worry not only about women going around in less underwear than in the fifties, but about their wearing no underwear at all. Bras, if they were to be worn, had to be minimal and pretty. By the end of the sixties, padded bras (often any bra) and all girdles were viewed with suspicion. They tampered with nature. We liked the "truth in packaging" approach even if the truth wasn't a perfect figure. My, my, how times had changed.

Sixties bathing suits continued and refined the pared-down trend of the fifties. Brigitte Bardot's St.-Tropez look, a gingham bikini with the bra cups underwired into rigid and undisguised half-moons, was *the* with-it look. One-piecers were okay but seemed modest in comparison. To wear one was to have something to hide. To show off the midriff was a statement of freedom.

Gradually both one-piece and two-piece suits benefited from technological developments in synthetic elastics. Spandex and Lycra stretched better, weighed less, smelled less, and permitted less cumbersome designs. Maillots were form-fitting—and their form was our form. The bra section was much less rigid and pre-constructed, than a few years before. Bikini tops evolved from molded circles to two triangles and some string.

As bizarre as sixties clothes and makeup were, hairdos were even freakier. Bigger was better. Bigger was called "bouffant." A

*Bikini tops in 1970 were rigidly shaped cups with obvious boning underneath.
They seemed daring at the time, but in retrospect they were almost demure.
(Jantzen, Inc.)*

rat's nest of hair was combed every which way until it stuck out,
and the top layer was smoothed over the mess. Hirsute helmets. We
all had our favorite brand of hair spray with its ideal combination of
sweet scent and sticking power. Hair spray stock was a good investment; we each went through an aerosol can a week. (We didn't
know about the ozone layer.)

The bouffanting process went by many names. Backcombing

and teasing sounded more refined than ratting. The term "ratting" came from the rattail comb whose thin handle was used to poke into the hairdo and lift it higher. Bouffants couldn't be brushed or combed during the day. They had to be lifted.

One early sixties style was the flip, a bouffant crown that curved into a smooth mono-curled bottom. The flip was worn with bangs, with headbands, and best of all, with both. Then beehives began to appear. We should have known that a hairstyle called the beehive was bound to be unbecoming. Then we cut our hair shorter and ratted it into a ball on top. Now we had a shorter hirsute helmet. The more moderate do was called the bubble. Still big and round, it had a definition of curls and was softer and more flattering. Vidal Sassoon brought a geometric element to hairstyles. His cuts were straight and swinging and at odds with the teased-to-the-nth-degree fad. They often hung over one eye. Sassoon's was Mary Quant's look, Twiggy's look, and (in a Joan of Arc version) Mia Farrow's "statement."

Soon our own hair wasn't enough. By 1965, Dynel wigs and falls were anchored on our heads. Wigs were easy to clean, easy to care for, cheap, and respectable. Some of us didn't show our real hair for years. When we did (mostly because we perceived the wig had become passé rather than from any personal disenchantment), it was quite an adjustment to return to real hair that was too thin, too curly, too unmanageable, or too oily. From long falls with built-up crowns for added height (the Marlo Thomas look) to short bubbles (the Harpo look) wigs, we thought, were wonderful. For the longest time the artificiality didn't bother us. We truly believed we had improved on nature.

Yves St. Laurent, despite his penchant for luxury fabrics and exotic inspirations, was a moderating influence in the sixties. He knew that we were acting like bratty children and needed some sense of limits. Quant, Courrèges, Gernreich wanted to push to the limit. St. Laurent kept us from going over the edge. He offered us some alternatives like the pea jacket, a classic in a nonclassic time. It was navy, not pea green (little did we know its name came from the Dutch *pij,* the word for coarse wool). St. Laurent's jacket wasn't coarse. It was of soft wool, elegant yet casual. Big bucks. The ones we found in the Army and Navy surplus stores were of coarse wool (and little bucks).

St. Laurent's foremost moderation measure was the pantsuit. Just when we reached rock bottom in silliness, we were shaken to our senses. "Now the girls have it all," *Life* proclaimed, referring to the new, high-fashion pants and jacket enesembles. The magazine advised that pantsuits be worn "with sturdy shoes and lots of long hair."

The suits, St. Laurent's and otherwise, were adaptions of man-tailoring. In 1966, they were selling like crazy in wool, double knit, and velvet. Pants ended at the ankle, a tentative move downward. Jackets covered the hip snugly and were often double-breasted. They were slicked-up men's jackets. Tailoring was everything. For the most part, pantsuits were elegant and lean.

Still, we couldn't wear them everywhere at first. *Time* magazine told us that pantsuits were not "as yet right for all places and occasions." A Manhattan socialite confided to the magazine's reporter that she hesitated to wear her new pantsuit unless she knew that "two other women will be wearing them. I hate to stand out." Women were refused tables at posh restaurants. Their femininity was questioned from all quarters. Would men learn to accept them in this new garb?

Converts were legion. The comfort of pantsuits was undeniable. Those years in miniskirts had been liberating but difficult. Pantsuits became a way of life. Once matching tailored jackets and pants opened up the whole question of women's choice to wear pants in general, less-tailored outfits became part of the whole pants scene too. The same jeans and capris that went to the market, the study hall, and the park now went to class, to work, to weddings, and to church.

It didn't happen overnight. Schools and businesses had dress codes. To turn up in a pantsuit at work often meant being refused admittance or being sent home to change, like an erring child. *Laugh-In*'s Judy Carne knew how to make a well-needed point as well as get a little publicity. She arrived at "21" in New York in a tunic and pants outfit and was refused a table. Judy's photographer recorded her solution: She slipped off the pants and strode past the *maître d'* in an acceptable micromini. The management got the point and the no-pants-on-women dictum was rescinded the next day.

Amy Vanderbilt cautioned *Ladies Home Journal* readers on the propriety of pantsuits. "High-heeled pumps, dangling earrings, fancy coiffures, and dainty handbags tend to look wrong with pantsuits." She may have known her salad fork from her elbow, but she was no fashion visionary. Lest we get carried away by our newfound freedom, Vanderbilt reminded us that "well-mannered men can also be a guide to women new to pants. A man with good manners does not put his trousered legs up on desks or other furniture, or put them higher than his head." Higher than his head? Whatever could she have meant? She added that we should bear in mind how "Oriental women have walked, sat, and moved through the centuries of pantswearing—in a very feminine fashion."

Most women wore pantsuits but not exclusively. The mini was still a viable alternative. By the end of the sixties, the miniskirt had permeated fashion to an astonishing degree. No woman this side of fifty or a size 16 was immune to its supposed charms. Gloria Steinem, who had great legs, and Jackie Kennedy, who didn't, wore them in public. While the micromini (which could be described as a skirt or skirtette able to cover your underpants only while you were standing perfectly straight) became the uppermost extent of the fad, any skirt that ended above the knees qualified as a mini. Qualifying as mini wearers were nurses (how they could make a bed with hospital corners and retain their dignity is a mystery) and grandmothers who would never have predicted they would reveal so much so late in life. (Were any grandmothers buried in their minis? A strangely disquieting thought.)

We became blind to the mini's shortcomings. We learned to walk, sit, pick things up off the floor with new deliberation. We suffered frozen kneecaps in winter. We went to job interviews dressed as go-go dancers.

By 1969, department stores were frantically trying to get a feel for how much longer the mini would be in style. The seers said, "No end in sight," and stores reordered heavily. Suddenly Parisian designers dropped their bomb. The hemline had always been their ultimate weapon. They deployed it without warning, throwing both stores and customers into confusion. "Something had to be done about the length," Marc Bohan told *Time.* "They couldn't get any shorter and besides, it's fun." Perhaps fun at first for the couturier-as-God who expected every fashion decree to be carried out by unquestioning devotees.

Mini. Midi. Maxi. Too much to choose from for women unaccustomed to such alternatives. In general, they reacted by buying the maxi only as a coat (those frozen kneecaps did not go unnoticed), rejecting the midi altogether, and turning to pants. The mini did not die a quick death with the designers' snap of the fingers. It was well into the seventies before women were willing to give them up.

The fact that the end of the mini didn't come until women were ready to give them up reflected power shifts in the clothing world. The authority of the couturier was crumbling. It was as if we had been unionized or politicized and believed that "if we all stick together, we can keep the mini, reject the midi, and crush the dictatorial power of the oppressive male designer-masters."

That such an important issue as self-determination in how we look should be waged over the mini was curious. The mini made us feel uncomfortable, cold, tense, and often just plain silly-looking, but we never cried, "Stop! We're being manipulated here." We merely asked, "How much shorter do you want it?"

Yes, the sexiness of miniskirts assured us that we, as the wearers, were in control of our destiny. If nothing else, we felt young in the mini. Maybe we didn't get millions of dates or have to fight off the hordes, but we still felt young. We perceived the midi as making us look old, when life was becoming increasingly youth oriented. We knew how the world was divided: Young was beautiful and old was ugly.

The midi was presented to us all wrong. It was an ultimatum: Wear it or else you'll look dated, old-fashioned, out of sync. Paris had issued edicts before, but the hemlines varied an inch or three one way or the other, and to disobey was not so blatant an act of rebellion. We were being told to chuck the whole closet. You couldn't turn minis into midis by letting down the hems. We needed an extra two feet of length, not two inches. It was a real fashion fiasco, with both sides fighting for authority. We were lucky to have pantsuits to wear while we worked the situation out and hippie regalia to divert our attentions.

The hippie look started out as a political statement, an anti-fashion, and then became the fashion itself. It went from a gesture of protest by the disenchanted and disenfranchised to a cultivated look for those who wanted to be "with it." The look fell into two categories: real hippie and rich hippie.

Beatnik had never been the fashion force that hippie evolved into. Beatnik was a limited style of dress with a limited palette: black. We loved black tights and turtlenecks, but they got a bit boring as daily wear. Hippie was just the opposite. It was never limited and the palette was kaleidoscopic. Hippie was limited only by our own imaginations.

The core of the look, real or rich, was jeans. Faded jeans were unassuming, common, the consummate antifashion in their natural state, all those qualities the original flower children wanted to project. The studding, painting, embroidering, stitching, patching came later, when it was no longer enough to be antifashion. You had to be antifashion with a vengeance.

The perfect, unassuming tops for faded jeans were blue work-shirts, sleeveless undershirts, and Wallace Beery shirts. Soon plain shirts, like plain jeans, weren't enough, and they were tossed in the washing machine with a box of Rit dye. The hippie look was one of evolution as well as revolution. At first, a plain undershirt was a strong statement in itself. No one had worn them as outer fashion before. They became too prosaic and needed to be dyed purple to say the same thing that plain undershirts could have said the year before. Then they had to be tie-dyed. Concentric circles and undu-lating line, psychedelic colors.

Once the anything-goes concept caught on, we took it literally

This still from the movie Hair *shows three sanitized versions of the hippie look: Indian print fabrics, long patchwork skirts, boots, scarves, rings, feathers, and bells.* (United Artists Corporation)

(as well as the nothing-goes corollary of nudity). Fashion was a visual candy store. Not just red with orange or blue with green, but red and orange and blue and green all together. Out of sight. The more brilliant, the better. Every item was brought to its wildest possible extension. Hats had the biggest, floppiest brims possible. Vests had three-foot-long fringes with beading all around. Nothing matched. We weren't wearing matching black purses and shoes those days. We chose beaded moccasins and Peruvian knitted bags. It was a one-from-column-A-one-from-column-B. And the more columns the better. It was a braless, girdleless, pantyhoseless life. No fashion magazines could instruct us in the hippie look. With the hippie look we had to turn to each other for inspiration. We found inspiration at protest rallies, Jimi Hendrix concerts and love-ins. We saw people in Indian block-print bedspread dresses, gypsy finery, fur-lined Afghani vests and coats, Nehru jackets, American Indian headbands, and, above all, beads. Cheap beads, junky beads. Love beads. To look more hippie, we just added more beads. The look was funky.

In all their variations, hippie clothes were still the uniform of the dropouts, the disillusioned, and the dilettantes versus the plastic, warmongering establishment. We had to let the world know which side we were on, even if we couldn't keep a job or have a civil conversation with our parents because of it. We rejected the straight world's values and that included its concept of proper dress. It was all very unkempt and unconventional but it was real, until Seventh Avenue got wind of a money-making trend. Too much revenue was being lost to Army-Navy surplus stores, Goodwill, and import shops. By the end of the sixties, rich hippie supplanted real hippie. There were fringed vests at Macy's and secondhand jeans at Gimbels. Seventh Avenue made the hippie look accessible and acceptable to millions. It also homogenized it, sanitized it, and obliterated the message behind the look.

The sixties were a period of aberration, but there were always some people who dressed sanely. When Jackie was wearing her simple suits and pillboxes, they wore their Villagers. When the mods turned out in microminis, they wore their Villagers. When the hippies sported faded jeans and ethnic tops and love beads, they wore their Villagers. There was a minor but continuing conservative strain all through the sixties, although it never made the front pages. Their shirtdresses were shorter than they might have been if the women hadn't felt any social pressure (but longer than the rest of the world's). Jumpers, slacks, safari jackets, Garland cardigans, button-down shirts, bulky mohair sweaters—somebody was still buying them. Luci Johnson stuck to her conservative Texas dressing, wearing saddle shoes in the White House. She didn't jump on the mod or hippie bandwagon. Neither did a lot of other women.

But there was no joy in Mudville; mighty Villager had struck

Sears' late sixties version of the Villager look came in shorter skirt lengths just like the real Villager clothes. It was the conservative Ivy League dresser's only accommodation to the mini-mod look. This was safe, but also merely dressing when everyone else was expressing herself. (Sears, Roebuck and Company)

The correct, hipbone-length Jackie Kennedy suit jacket and overblouse with princess seams is worn with simple (but uncomfortable) pumps, gloves, and a dead-center pin. (Universal Pictures Company)

out. Wearing Evan-Picone meant just wearing clothes when every woman about you was expressing herself. There were problems with being sane in an insane world.

In the summer of 1961, we all bought shirtwaist dresses in "guaranteed to bleed" Madras and talked about what a "good transitional outfit" they'd be. Oh, the rigidity of the change of seasonal wardrobes, after Memorial Day and Labor Day.

—*M. Miller*

To cut off the waistband, Peter Pan or button-down collar, long or short sleeves, and full skirts—all in favor of the sleeveless, bateau neck, dropped waist, figure-skimming shift—was to achieve the last word in elegance. Add to this the low, chunky-heeled pump and just the right pin in the center or off to the side of one's upper bodice—well, we are talking a million-dollar look. Need you ask the inspiration?

—Nancy Kinney

I made my own clothes when I started to work as a librarian. They were beautiful clothes, beautifully made but so very serious. It's hard to believe I ever wore anything so formal and conservative as those suits and Jackie Kennedy A-line dresses. So neat and trim. I was living in Washington, married, and working during Kennedy's administration. I'm sure I was influenced by her, but also already impatient with neat dresses and stockings and heels.

—Peggy Byrnes

Jackie Kennedy's style formed the taste I had as a just-married woman in the sixties. Never mind that we all looked like we had paper-doll-flat, stiff cutout clothes latched on our shoulders with flat tabs—it seemed *adult* compared to skirts and sweaters.

—Sara B. Chase

During the Camelot years, I was definitely influenced by Jackie Kennedy's style. Lacking the Kennedy millions, I could still buy a pillbox hat or two.

—Carolyn Zucker

Junior high graduation stands out in my mind, for clothing was the most important aspect to us. Every girl had to have a wool knit suit (set by the girls), and I think the rule was that we all had to wear high-heeled shoes—those pointy two-inch pumps. I shopped around and finally found a pretty light turquoise suit. It was so uncomfortable for a fourteen-year-old. Also a pair of heels that I (along with all the girls) barely waddled across the stage in. My biggest worry was tripping. The suit was a straight skirt (lined), a shell top, and a jacket. Something I would feel mature in, even today. I loved being so adult, but I hated being so confined. I don't think I ever wore that suit again. Or the shoes either.

—Susan Stern

Some of us copied the Jackie Kennedy look more successfully than others. A model pulled it off with her figure-skimming suit. The sleeves are a Jackie-prescribed three-quarter length with the gloves filling in the lower arm. The shoes and hairdo are restrained and ladylike. Surely the hatbox is filled with pillboxes. (Gloria List)

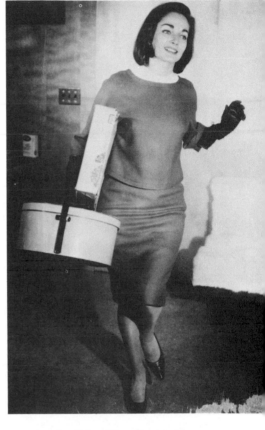

With those pointy toes on shoes, no wonder I have bunions today.
—*Gloria List*

Must mention those killer pointy-toed, pencil-heeled shoes of the sixties. Ugh! And yet the mincing along seemed to feel so feminine.
—*Sara B. Chase*

Pointy-toe shoes were always uncomfortable. Yet I *loved* them.
—*Emby Searson*

I hated pointy shoes. They were so painful.
—*Regina Neuman*

The Jackie look for evening: a simple bateau neckline, sleeveless black dress. The severity of the dress was cut by the frou-frou stole. Models in those days did a lot of posing in one-legged stork positions. (Gloria List)

I loved pointy-toe pumps. The more pointed, the better. I thought round-toe shoes looked like old lady shoes or baby shoes. Now I wear them exclusively. I wouldn't think of buying pointy-toe shoes today.

—Lyn Messner

An electrician's daughter couldn't even ask for Villager clothes. J. C. Penney's was considered the norm. So I went to work at my sewing machine, night after night. It was tedious trying to copy those Villager fashions. The prints had to be tiny little soft pastel flowers of 100 percent cotton, and of course the wools had to be heathered soft shades. I labored meticulously and successfully copied every detail, including the buttons they used. The real way to know a Villager blouse was the seam that was used on the armhole, a kind of flat-fell seam without the topstitching. It was a terror to achieve, but desperation had a way of guiding me on to ultimate success. That was the beginning of my sewing career and my virtual obsession with wonderful clothes.

—Barbara Diamond

It was at the University of Pennsylvania that I learned the true meaning of John Meyer of Norwich, Villager, and Pappagallo. Since my suitemates in college decided that I was a perfect size to fit them, I had to spruce up my clothing to fit the mode. After Thanksgiving vacation, I tossed out the hippie look and brought in the Villager look. We all shared a common wardrobe.

—Laurie Burrows Grad

The biggest status of all in those years was owning an entire wardrobe of Villager clothing. We were, of course, the original preppies then, which is why I am amazed that the Pasadena brigade, mature women in their thirties and forties, could ever consider doing the same look again. Villager clothing was identifiable even to amateurs: little rounded collars, all shirts made of 100 percent cotton, guaranteed to wrinkle. Heathered woolens with coordinated cable-stitch heather sweaters. Bermudas with front flies (sure to put twenty pounds on the best of us) and heavy woolen pants with the same fly front. Those little round-collared shirts came in every color of the rainbow and I desperately wanted one for my very own, but in 1963 they cost $8. Apparently that was an astronomical amount of money because I remember grabbing some up (my first treasures) on sale for $4, knowing my mother couldn't complain about that.

—Barbara Diamond

While studying in Europe, most of the other students at my school were from New England and I was introduced to "true prep." I liked it and felt comfortable in the fresh, casual look and still do. The problem, at the time, was that such clothes weren't available in southern California. I really feel that this look was meant for me.

—Lyn Messner

The All-American-Girl look in 1960. The newest Gidget poses in the perfect, conservative, Middle America outfit. The Bermuda-collared (not to be con- fused with Peter Pan) shirt is buttoned to the top. The plaid wool skirt with stitched-down pleats was coordinated with a plain jacket. Any sixteen-year-old would have done the dishes for a month for an outfit like this. (Columbia Pic- tures)

In 1960–1964, I can remember salivating as I watched the wealthy girls of Arlington, Virginia, Wakefield High School saunter down the halls in their Madras plaid shirts (guaranteed to bleed—if they didn't bleed, they were fake and second class) and their Bass Weejuns (loafers), which everybody knew were Bass because they had the notch cut into the section where the penny or nickel was inserted. I had the hardest time explaining to my mother that the notch was crucial. She never did let me buy them.

—Barbara Diamond

In high school I lived on the south shore of Long Island in a town called Bay Shore (a very middle-to-upper-middle WASP neighborhood). I had an entire wardrobe of Villager and John Meyer. Everything was color-coordinated: button-down oxfords, A-line skirts, and cardigan sweaters. The important feature was that each outfit had a coordinating bangle bracelet, a thin grosgrain ribbon for my hair (tied in a perfect bow), and a canvas golf-ball bag that I used as a pocketbook. I had one in every color. Villager taught me how to get four outfits out of every two. This is a skill I have never lost.

—Tristine Berry

Monogrammed everything was considered *trés chic* in college, 1964–1965. First essential was a monogrammed pin with your three initials. If it was carved out, it was obviously a better quality than if it was just stenciled into a plain round solid pin. Handbags had initials. ID bracelets, ankle bracelets (like the guy wouldn't know you if you didn't have your initials on your ankle bracelet), but the ultimate initialing was to have sweaters with gorgeous big initials smack in the center of your chest. And then to have your little round-collared oxford shirt closed at the neck by your three-initial pin. In those days the other ultimate jewelry trend (this was on a college campus, the University of Cincinnati) was to wear as many pins over your heart as possible. These would be membership pins to any and *all* of the following: sorority, honor societies, clubs, religious organizations. And of course if a girl was actually "pinned" by her boyfriend with his fraternity or honor society pin, she would find that just putting on her pins could make her late for an early morning class. Usually the pins had two parts. To make matters even sillier, they were connected with a fine chain so there were pins and chains overlapping each other, and the more one had, the more "in" one appeared to be. I loved it all and attempted to wear every damn one of them. Talk about identity crisis!

—*Barbara Diamond*

The oxford-cloth shirts popular in college were a nuisance to iron, so we used to just press the parts that showed—the collar and the cuffs.

—*Linda Finch*

When I was in college, I remember a girl down the hall who used to iron just the collar and front of her Villager oxford shirts because she wore a V-necked, long-sleeved loose sweater over them. I thought she was gross not to iron the whole shirt, when I was spending hours with my spray starch and iron getting every wrinkle out.

—*Barbara Diamond*

My first mini was a then-daring 1½ inches above the knee, worn with fishnet pantyhose.

—*Manuela Cerruti*

As for minis, I remember one incident. I was writing for a rhythm-and-blues newspaper called *Soul*. The soul singer, James Brown, invited me to join him on a tour of the West Coast, flying with him in his Lear jet. Brown was a real mystery character. I was thrilled and not a little scared to be with him in such close quarters. We boarded the plane and he ushered me to the seat directly across from him. I sat down, he sat down, and then he got up, unfolded a newspaper, and laid it across my miniskirted legs. "That's the problem with those miniskirts," he said, resuming his seat.

—*Rochelle Reed*

I had many minis. My funniest image was my Zsa Zsa Gabor (in reverse) experience. In 1965, my husband, Joe, and I had just left Paris, and Givenchy, and headed for a small farm in Hungary to meet his European relatives for the first time. His Baba Yaga bent-over aunt, in her seventies, wearing a babushka and a long, flowered peasant skirt with many aprons, was excitedly walking me through her farm, pointing out pigs, peonies, fruits, and nuts. I was walking

All the models in Mademoiselle's *August college issue were coeds. They posed (usually on campus) wearing the magazine's suggestions on what to wear to class in September. This 1966 layout recommended a Carnaby look minidress and textured pantyhose.* (Condé Nast)

through mud, leaves, and assorted animal droppings wearing high-heeled black leather knee boots that fit like a glove, a black leather miniskirt, a blue-black Austrian wool turtleneck sweater, rings on nearly every finger, and a collection of bracelets almost to my elbow. As I looked back at the thatched-roof house, I saw a line of silent, gaping relatives and neighbors staring at me. I was the first American woman they'd ever met and probably sporting the most exposed legs they'd ever seen in public. They thought I was hilariously funny. I thought I'd been dropped back in a historical time capsule. They giggled and treated me royally, knowing full well that a woman who looked like that could obviously do nothing on a farm.

—Anne Wehrer

For a few years, lace pantyhose and fishnet tights were considered perfectly respectable, perfectly ladylike. A while later, they were deemed strictly for hookers. (Sears, Roebuck and Company)

I had a beautiful turquoise shift with a ruffled front that I loved to wear to work. I was sure it was utterly becoming on me. On one occasion I was visiting a gypsy family (I am a social worker) and the teenage children were complimenting me on the dress. Their mother looked me over critically and sniffed, "Don't you think that dress is too small?"

—Dawn Sturgill

I'm not sure we ever got used to minis even though we wore them. You could always date a woman by how many times she kept pulling down that skirt that disappeared when she sat down. We seemed to think that if we tugged hard enough, it would cover our knees. Now I blush to think of standing up in front of a class of junior lechers with half my thighs showing.

—Nancie L. Porter

On Madison Avenue in New York, I was crossing the street wearing my high-fashion, slick white plastic miniskirt with white Courrèges boots. I overtook an octogenarian matron with a caked, cracked, white-powdered face, red lipstick trying in vain to define lost lips, and slightly blue-tinted hair. I heard her begin to sputter unintelligible curses, interpersed with recognizable phases: "What is this world coming to?" "Disgusting!" and "Go back to Forty-second Street where you belong!"

I felt unjustifiably attacked. After all, I'd grown up on that block in the same social set, always flaunting the fashion of the time. Her last gasp was a fit of cane-shaking anger, climaxed by a huge gob of spit that *landed* on my skirt. My astonishment gave way to pity as we stepped up on the curb, facing our reflections in a shop mirror. The contrast was too much. In her eyes, I was obscene. In mine, I was *avant-garde*.

—Anne Wehrer

I wore miniskirts so short that I wore Danskin panties over my pantyhose.

—Emby Searson

In the late sixties I wore minis along with everyone else. Working in an architect's office, I quickly realized that my bending over the

Minis were fine for walking (except up outside stairwells), but much less fine for sitting. A midthigh mini of respectable length became a micromini when the wearer took a seat. It required certain survival techniques to keep one's dignity. This woman has learned the best place for her purse—as sort of a paperweight. Men welcomed the mini as a chance to catch crotch shots, but mini-wearers thwarted them at every turn. Except for those stairwells. (American Broadcasting Company)

drafting board in my mini was creating some comment. My first solution was ruffled tennis shorts, à la Gussie Moran. Worn under pantyhose, the ruffles were smashed. Worn outside, they were bulky. There was really no good solution, though I settled for two pairs of underpants—one under the pantyhose, the other on top.
                                                                            —*Gloria Casvin*

Having worn minis all through the sixties and into the seventies, I developed a mode of sitting, standing, and kneeling . . . an entire way of life that was unique to the miniskirt. For instance: you *never* bent over to pick up something off the ground. A specialized technique had to be used to get your hand down far enough to grasp the

desired item without revealing all to everyone. I would press my
knees tightly together and place my feet about five-six inches apart.
In this position I leaned to the side, slowly swaying my knees in the
opposite direction. My shoulders would lower (on the side I was
leaning), and my hand would swoop down and snare the desired ob-
ject off the ground. Of course, this took great dexterity and muscu-
lar control, not to mention how embarrassing it was when I failed.

—*Pamela J. Baergen*

Miniskirts—the shorter, the better. I met and married my husband
dressed in white boots and a miniskirt.

—*Laurie Burrows Grad*

I went to teach at Penn State University in 1966 and wore miniskirts and fishnet stockings to my freshman composition class. Good
grief!

—*Sara B. Chase*

After college the miniskirts really caught on. I was teaching then,
and I remember checking out a skirt's appropriateness for wearing
when writing on the board by raising my arms to see how high it
would rise up.

—*Linda Finch*

Skirts were getting shorter, but all I remember about minis was
going to an interview in Pasadena. It was for an administrative job,
and I wore a blue dress trimmed with a white collar that I had
turned into a minidress. The horror of seeing it hanging in the closet
a few years later. How could I have worn it to an interview? I didn't
get the job.

—*Peggy Byrnes*

Minis were ghastly. No one ever looked good in them. I burned
every picture I ever had. Boys and men liked them.

—*Sandy Whitehurst*

I liked wearing the mini because I felt good in it. This was before
my feminist days. People, mostly boys, would make comments about
how good I looked and it made me feel great. Thinking back on it

This perfectly respectable dress in its time looks like hooker garb today. In the late sixties, women wore dresses like this to job interviews. Except for the length and the provocative pose, it's really a rather demure dress with a ladylike slip underneath, dressy T-strap pumps, and a tiny, conservative handbag. (Seven Arts Associated Productions)

now, it's pretty clear that I dressed for approval from men. Although lots of times it was uncomfortable wearing short skirts, I knew the reaction I would elicit and I dressed for that reaction.
—*Sandy Calin*

In college I cut off all my wool skirts to midthigh length.
—*Lyn Messner*

I was working as a switchboard operator during the miniskirt years. I sat on a high stool and tucked my dress under me. Then I had to remember to keep my knees together when I swung around and faced the room. Every time I reached up to plug or unplug a call, I

Men's fantasies of what life-with-the-mini would be were scotched by women's determination to retain their dignity as much as possible (of course, it was not always possible). Panty-slips were one method. (Sears, Roebuck and Company)

would have to redo my neat little tucked mini. It was reach-and-tuck, reach-and-tuck all night, week in and week out. I *had* to be stylish even if it was a pain. I couldn't let a stocking top, a garter, a girdle cuff, or (finally) the panty part of the pantyhose show for even a second. It was draining.

—Ellen Ekman

Miniskirts were the most important fashion statement in my life. They came into vogue just as I was beginning to discover clothes and boys. I was living back east, in Virginia, when I finally convinced my mother to let me wear a mini. It was 1968, and I'd been hiking up my skirts after I left the house for school for two years. My mother was rather reluctant to see me wear skirts eight inches above my knees, to put it mildly. I was in junior high school, and I believed that everyone else in the entire world could wear short skirts except me.

I knew I had to wear minis after I saw Twiggy on TV and in magazine layouts. More important, somehow I managed to see her live in a fashion show in Washington, D.C., in 1968, and that *really* did it. Not only did I want short skirts, I wanted lots of eye makeup too (especially long eyelashes).

After 1969, when my family moved to California, my mother gave up on fighting short skirts. In high school my girl friends and I wore skirts that barely covered our little butts. It was a matter of pride—the skirts had to be short, but not so short as to have us sent home.

—Alice Short

The first miniskirt I wore was in college, 1966–1967. Before that, I would roll up my skirts to make them shorter. In college I went for the scissors. It really is a joke because there really isn't anything attractive about the look.

—Tristine Berry

In my rush to get into New York from the Washington, D.C., commuter plane, I quickly grabbed my suitcase—one of a dozen look-a-like bags. At home I discovered a gray flannel business suit, boxer shorts, a tie, black socks, a Brooks Brothers button-down shirt, and assorted toiletry articles—pure corporate-image attire.

In his hotel (God forbid his home!), he found my Andy War-holesque wardrobe. (I was making a film with Warhol at the time.) It included a silver plastic miniskirt, a glittery silver sweater with matching stockings, silver spike heels, and silver, slinky, kinky un-derclothing from Frederick's. Either he went casual to his meeting, or in drag. If at home, he went to his lawyer.

—Anne Wehrer

When I began working as a social worker for Los Angeles County, I wore my miniskirts in the office. The personnel manager made a personal comment to me about the shortness of my dress when I was first hired, which surprised me, because I did have an idea about how to "dress for success." That particular dress was one of my longest! I did have a designer minidress, though, which was shorter than my present-day tennis skirts.

—Dawn Sturgill

The best thing that happened to me in terms of clothes is that Rudi Gernreich, Emilio Pucci, and Calvin Klein were all designing. Rudi Gernreich's clothes were carried out of a wonderful store on Wil-shire Boulevard in Beverly Hills called Jax. I think the Gernreich clothes got me married . . . they were skinny and spare when every-body else was voluminous . . . and for me, "chic" was invented to describe him.

I'll never forget the first Pucci that I owned . . . way out of my price range at the time, but then there never was and never will be anything like those skimpy little dresses with the Empire waists in the incredible colors. A miracle of sexiness and design. I have put away my favorite Pucci to be buried in.

I never minded all those petticoats and remember traveling once on promotion for Catalina swimsuits with a suitcase that held noth-ing *but*. It was hell getting on and off trains with so much luggage. But for the most part, I loved the sleek, pared-down look and still do.

—Helen Gurley Brown

I went through an extended op art phase, always black and white and dizzy-busy. I deliberately wore these costumes to op art shows. I got hooked on black and white and wore only those two colors (or all black clothes) for a period of five years. This made accessories easy, and decisions minimal. It helped to be tall and thin with an "attitude." I carried it all the way: black-and-white tights, white lipstick, and black-and-white hair. I worked at being conspicuous within the good taste of dynamite fabric and design. I loved the performance aspect of this period. Over the years I built up a reputation to uphold. Once I said to one of my teenage daughters, "Please let me know if I am carrying this extreme fashion-costume play too far—to the point of being ridiculous." Paula said, "Mom, it's too late."

—Anne Wehrer

I remember panty girdles in the ninth grade, in 1962. We wore straight skirts and without a girdle your fanny would move. Considered very crude. In the late seventies we all wore straight skirts with our suits—and never considered a panty girdle. Interesting.

—Tristine Berry

We had to wear girdles because God forbid someone should see something move.

—Rose Mary Kimble

Before girdles had back seams to "lift and separate." I remember seeing women wearing girdles under pants. They looked monobottomed, much like women of the 1890s looked monobosomatic.

—Nancy Kinney

When I was working at Disney Studios in 1969, I saw Julie Andrews walking down the hall one day. I remember thinking that I'd never seen a woman look so elegant in pants. It was not only the cut of the pants but the fact that she had no VPL. Remember, VPL was not merely the line around the legs but the hipline, as well as the half-moon in the back of the crotch.

—Nancy Kinney

We wore bikinis in 1963. They weren't quite as abbreviated at first as what I remember seeing in *Life* (on the Riviera), but they got briefer and briefer as the summers went by. Growing up in southern California meant I spent a lot of time at the beach during the summer. Most of my clothes reflected that—a zippered sweat shirt, cot-

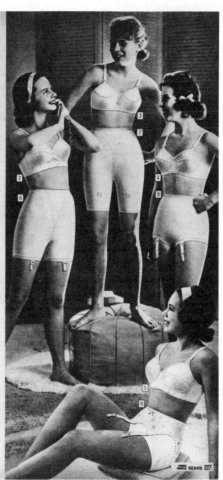

YOUNG FIGURES

[1] **Effa Cordtex®** inserts in cups give gentle lift. Prettily embroidered uppercups. Fine cotton in well-designed teen bra. Elastic inserts in front band and at back hooks. Straps adjust. White.

Catalog No.	Cup	State bra size
18 H 24302F	Teen AA	30, 32, 34, 36
18 H 24313F	Teen A	30, 32, 34, 36
18 H 24324F	Teen B	32, 34, 36, 38

Shpg. wt. ea. 3 oz....$1.89...2 for $3.70...3 for $5.40

[2] **Rotation stitched cups.** Elastic inserts in doubled front band, at 3-way back hooks. Straps adjust. White cotton. Made in Jamaica. Wt. ea. 4 oz.

Catalog No.	Cup	State bra size
18 H 24902F	Teen AA	30, 32, 34, 36
18 H 46803F	Regular A	32, 34, 36, 38

$1.49....2 for $2.94....3 for $4.35....4 for $5.60

[3] **Cups give light support** to the figure just developing. White cotton with elastic inserts at front and at 2-way back hooks. Shpg. wt. ea. 4 oz. Teen AA-cup. State bra size 28, 30, 32, 34, 36, 38
18 H 24822F—97c......................3 for $2.85

[4] **Light contour of foam rubber** gives a smooth line. Lower cups are stitched, upper embroidered. Wide elastic center gore. All cotton. White.

Catalog No.	Cup	State bra size
18 H 24332F	Teen AA	30, 32, 34, 36
18 H 43233F	Regular A	32, 34, 36

Shpg. wt. ea. 6 oz....................97c...3 for $2.79

[5] **Lustre Stitch®** in lower cups gives you a light uplift. Elastic inserts in front and at 2-way back hooks. Straps adjust. All white cotton.

Catalog No.	Cup	State bra size
18 H 24122F	Teen AA	30, 32, 34, 36
18 H 49153F	Regular A	30, 32, 34, 36, 38

Shipping wt. ea. 3 oz...............97c...3 for $2.85

WonderS-P-A-N knit elastic (nylon, spandex) stretches two ways to gently smooth teen figures. 4 garters detach; hidden on long leg panty. Self fabric crotch. Machine wash, dry. White.
► Average Hips, 8 to 10 in. larger than waist. Small, medium, large. In waist sizes 24 to 30. State waist size.

[6] **Panty.** Fits about 15 in. waist down.
18 H 1925F—Shipping weight 4 ounces.....$3.30
[7] **Long Leg Panty.** Fits about 18 in. waist down.
18 H 1928F—Shipping weight 6 ounces.....$3.80
[8] **Brief.** Fits about 12 in. waist down.
18 H 26923F—Shipping weight 6 ounces.....$2.85
[9] **Garter belt** is specially designed to fit the teenage figure. Pretty pink embroidery trims nylon sheer. Ribbon trim on narrow 2½-in. front. Back hooks. 4 garters adjust. White. Wt. ea. 4 oz.
► In even waist sizes 22 to 28. State waist size.
18 H 721132F...........$1.40...2 for $2.70...3 for $3.90

Just say "Charge It"
and pay later .. see page 707-708

SEARS 227

Teenage girls were brainwashed into thinking they needed girdles, especially under straight skirts, so they wouldn't reveal any unsightly jiggles. With a full skirt, they could get away with a garter belt. Everything we wore underneath our clothes was white. (Sears, Roebuck and Company) ton shifts, sandals. We were all influenced by surfing styles. I started streaking my hair.

—*Lyn Messner*

My first two-piece bathing suit was Madras. It faded every time I wore it.

—*Michele Burgess*

In 1960, I was in the seventh grade and the vogue was sneakers and stockings. I had most colors in a corduroy fabric. Anything but white. My parents would not allow me to wear them. On one particular night there was a school dance that I was lucky enough to attend. Since my sneakers would not pass my parents' inspection at the door, I threw them out of my bedroom window. Problem was that it was snowing. I attended the dance and squished and squirted water all night. I was also one sick lady that next week.

—*Tristine Berry*

I remember all the clothes I wore for memorable dates, so they must have been important.

—*Joanna Wood*

Dressing for dates, you never knew what to wear. Dressy? Casual? You were always panicked about making the wrong choice. I remember one date about 1970. I put on a dress and heels for a night at the theater with a really nice, wealthy guy. I opened the door to find him wearing a sweat shirt. Neither one of us mentioned the disparity in our attire, not once during the evening.

—*Rose Mary Kimble*

I have vivid recollections of clothes in junior high because it was the time of rigid conformity to styles, which were set by the most popular girls. There was the bubble hairdo, which *everybody* had, ratted and sprayed. But not too much so you wouldn't be like the cheap girls.

—*Susan Stern*

We wore beehive hairdos that stayed in place for days without moving a hair. We wrapped them up in tissue paper at night and looked like mummies. There were always stories about spiders and other bugs living inside those beehives.

—Emby Searson

I remember white lipstick painted on by itself or put over (or under) some atrocious pinkish color. Real garish. And ratted hair with a flip at the sides.

—Regina Neuman

Shu-Mak-Up was for suckers like me. I'd see the ads in the magazines and really believe that I could take an old pair of black flats and, with a little bottle of Shu-Mak-Up ("dries like nail polish"), turn them into emerald-green or hot-pink numbers. The shoes in the ads looked perfect. Not a crack, not a smudge. The Shu-Mak-Up people would have you believe you could do complicated patterns like gingham and plaid to match your clothes. Shu-Mak-Up-ed shoes may have looked good at fifty paces (or in the ads), but close-up they looked junky. You had to apply the paint very carefully so that not one drop touched the sole—but you had to get it so close to the sole that you couldn't see the old color. Impossible. You also had to get it inside the top, nice and neat, so if you slipped your shoes off in public, nobody would see a mess. The paint would crack and flake away around any old cracks (and what shoes didn't have cracks after a wearing or two?). But I kept trying. Plunking down $1.25 after $1.25. The promise of colored shoes—dozens of colors like tangerine, olive green, turquoise—was too great to resist. Perhaps it was an art form and I just expected perfection too soon.

—Ellen Ekman

I used QT lotion to give me a tan out of a bottle. Only it was never really tan. Sometimes it was green, sometimes orange. It got all over your hands so they were an orangy brown. It was hard to get the stuff to fade naturally into your regular skin color. It just ended. You never knew how far up the leg to put it so that no matter how far you bent over or crossed your leg, your pasty-white real color wouldn't show. You couldn't cover your whole body because the stuff was expensive. And it rubbed off on your clothes (and the sheets). QT on white bra straps looked disgusting. And where should you stop on your feet? You couldn't do your soles because

soles don't tan. So you wound up stopping just below the shoe line.
That meant you couldn't slip your shoes off. And the sandal situation was hopeless. It really never worked. It was always too much
trouble. But it took me a while to realize that.

—Emby Searson

In the early sixties, my husband-at-the-time bought me a Chanel
quilted handbag on one of his business trips to Paris. I loved wearing
it to the grocery store in Westport, Connecticut—with my blue
jeans.

—Gloria List

The very first day I got to college, not knowing any better, I
showed up in a red plaid minidress. That was the last time anyone
there saw my legs. It was shirts and jeans (or dungarees in New
York) all the way. The dungarees were all hip-huggers and bell-
bottomed. One day, at a college party, a couple of friends painted
my dungarees with signs and pictures in a Day-Glo paint. My
mother was scandalized.

—Manuela Cerruti

I used to wear pants so tight that I would get cramps. I loved stretch
pants with foot straps that pulled a little too tight. That way they
acted like a girdle and covered up any cellulite. I once shopped for
three days for the perfect pair of red stretch pants.

—Emby Searson

I remember hating ski pants or stretch pants even though I wore
them. They felt so tight and pulled on your waist and made me feel
fat because they were so small. They especially accented round
thighs, and inevitably they developed baggy knees after being worn
for half an hour.

—Regina Neuman

One needed good legs for stretch pants. I found them rather uncomfortable, but I noticed that men liked them.

—Sandy Whitehurst

Stretch pants came with stirrups to anchor them down and give the wearer a long, slim silhouette (though rarely as long and lean as on these models). We never bothered to hide the straps. Creases were stitched down the front for a permanent crispness. (Sears, Roebuck and Company)

When midiskirts and maxiskirts became fashionable, I was totally disappointed, and stopped wearing skirts and dresses altogether. For years I wore pants exclusively.

—*Manuela Cerruti*

After minis came midis, and I was always positive the designers did it so you would have to buy a new wardrobe. Everyone knows you can't let down the hem on a mini enough to turn it into a midi.

—*Michele Burgess*

Because we couldn't wear pants or shorts in the dining room commons, skirts were worn until after dinner. I can remember changing into wool shorts and knee socks to go to the library to study and socialize. My knees got so cold (northern Ohio can have nasty winters), but I felt with it.

—*Linda Finch*

Culottes felt very strange, like something was between my legs. But they were comfortable after you got used to them.

—*Marilyn Overholt*

I liked culottes because they allowed me to sit in class without having to remember to keep my legs together.

—*Beth Padon*

In California we had surfer pants as well as Bermuda shorts and pedal pushers. Surfer pants were cut off just above the knee.

—*Michele Burgess*

My all-time favorite piece of clothing—in which I always felt great—was a pair of navy wool knit pants. Very full in the leg but tapered out from the hip, not the knee. I wore it with a white, lacy, ruffled blouse. I got one of my favorite compliments in that outfit. I was waiting in front of my husband's office after work when one of the construction workers across the street yelled, "I would pay you a compliment on that but my whistle's broke." I was so sure of that outfit that I wore it to my ten year class reunion.

—*M. Miller*

In the sixties I remember it was scandalous when a girl in my college English class wore Bermuda shorts one very hot spring day. We were all amazed that she had such courage. It was just a normal class. People wore pants to school, but it was frowned upon if you wore them too often. Today a woman would have to wear a bikini to class to elicit such a response.

I also remember a friend of mine, a young woman in her early twenties, who was stopped by a school official on the campus of Santa Monica College. She had gone to register for a class and, without thinking, had worn slacks. She was married and the mother of a baby daughter and really wasn't expecting anyone to rule on her dress. But she was stopped and warned that she wasn't properly attired to be on a college campus.

Ten years later, in the late seventies, I was working for several Los Angeles and Beverly Hills law firms, and only one had a dress code. And they were considered behind the times because of the code. Women could wear pantsuits, but the jackets and pants had to match. And women were required to wear their jackets in the halls. In other firms many of the women, even women attorneys, not just clerical, wore faded jeans to work.

—Regina Neuman

Some of my friends used to wear the vinyl minis, and they had to be very careful where they sat or the vinyl would stick to some surfaces like plastic car seats. Vinyl was too noisy for my taste.

—Sandy Calin

If you were aware and hip, you wore bell bottoms. If you were a nerd, you didn't. My mother made me a pair of pink bell bottoms in 1968, and I used to wear them when I sneaked into Georgetown on the bus. I knew I couldn't hang out in Georgetown in a skirt that came below my knees! I wore the pink bell bottoms along with my brown leather peace sign, especially when I headed for Dupont Circle. Like miniskirts, bell bottoms eventually just became the expected dress and lost their political significance. When straight-legged pants became the vogue again, I can't say I missed the bell bottoms. They look a little silly to me now.

—Alice Short

In high school and college, winter coats with big fur collars were in. I got one of these when I went to college: camel wool with a red fox collar. By the end of college, I had become "aware" and wouldn't be caught wearing a dead animal around my neck. So I gave it to a cousin. Just a few years later, I regretted giving up that beautiful red fox.

—Gloria Casvin

High school—it was about this time that I became seriously hooked on fashion magazines. I remember buying the only copy of *Charm* (before *Glamour* took it over) in the local drugstore. I think I was influenced by these magazines more than I realized at the time. I recall my mother checking out *Vogue*s from our little local library. Did I mention that I grew up in an Iowa farming community of 1200 people?

—Annette Swanberg

During the late sixties it was very important to wear baggy clothes, especially men's clothes. My father was a career military man, and I thought his old wardrobe would be perfect for me. Unfortunately, he did not agree. We used to quarrel upon occasion because I wanted to wear his old flak jackets or uniform shirts and he refused to let me. So eventually I turned to wearing women's clothes that were several sizes too large, or boyfriends' shirts and sweaters. In the early seventies, when I was in high school, girls were allowed to wear pants to school when it rained. We had a complete uniform: men's cords (much too large), blue tennis shoes, and men's shirts.

—Alice Short

During my freshman year at UC Berkeley in 1968, a man's blue workshirt was one of the in clothing items on campus, and I wanted one in the worst way. Having one allowed you to be a number of things, depending on the occasion or circumstances. It was the most comfortable thing to study in, especially when worn by itself. Even the smallest men's size was too large and could be worn as a nightshirt. Of course, the radical dress in Berkeley was a workshirt and scruffy jeans. A year or two later, I discovered it could make one sexually appealing when again it was worn by itself. My boyfriend

teases me about clutching onto that old hippie image when I wear it
too often.

—*Pansy Yee*

The late sixties could best be called my bohemian stage, and my
dress reflected it. Black or navy tights were *de rigueur*. I wore
mostly black or other dark-colored miniskirts and pullover turtlenecks. I began to let my hair grow, and I parted it in the middle and
pulled it back with a dark scarf. When I was twenty, I traveled to
Europe, Israel, and Mexico, and I began to like ethnic jewelry.
From my trip to England in 1960, I remember my first clunky
shoes with fat high heels. I spent half my time in London looking for
shoes. They were so fascinating. I found a pair that were kind of old
English with a gorgeous antique-gold finish. They were so different
from the pointy-toe flats everyone had been wearing. When I came
home, the clunky style began to appear in Los Angeles, but I never
found a pair that I liked as much.

—*Susan Stern*

In Hawaii, hippie, earth mother, flower child all influenced me. No
prep at all. I made long skirts and dresses from paisley bedspread
fabric. I wore sandals all the time. I ate only health foods and discovered brown rice and yogurt. I listened to Joni Mitchell and let my
hair grow long and straight. No more rollers. No bra unless I felt
like it. Halter tops with embroidery or painted decoration. Beads
made of seeds. Big earrings. Rings. We went to the "Crater Festi-
vals," listened to rock bands, and meandered around doing whatever. I thought it was a wonderful time. I enjoyed the fun of
dressing in a way unlike anything I had ever worn.

—*Lyn Messner*

My first tie-dye was a Halston. A two-piece velour pantsuit. It was
gorgeous. I still have it but I never wear it. The colors are brown,
gold, and rust, and it has a wrap top that ties at the side. My husband-at-the-time bought it for me for Christmas at Halston in New
York. It cost $200, which was a great deal of money in 1969. Hal-
ston told my husband that "Jane Fonda just bought one like it," and
I think that cinched the deal for him.

—*Gloria List*

When tie-dye was part of hippie regalia, it seemed clever and artistic. But when it went mainstream, it lost its charm. This is the cover of a Rit "How to tie-dye" booklet that explained how to tie-dye practically everything in your closet. In more ways than one, it just didn't wash. (CPC Corporation)

Jeans were the basic building blocks of all hippie wardrobes. At first, they were simple and unadorned. Later they were painted, studded, patchworked, and embroidered. (Warner Brothers)

I thought I was the greatest when I'd dress up for a Beatles concert in my white half-boots, black stretch pants, black turtleneck sweater, white vinyl vest, and pebbled vinyl cloche hat. I wore this outfit everywhere—even to the Royal Ballet. When you're seventeen and think you've found the definitive outfit, even the mink coats at the Hollywood Bowl can't dampen your spirits.

—*Pamela J. Baergen*

Instead of fabric from the Home Silk Shop, I stopped in at the nearest import shop for Madras bedspreads from which to fashion skirts and dresses.

—*Linda Dahl*

Ah! The sixties! I look back on those years lovingly. Men in florid shirts and pants with scarves and beads. Myself in tie-dye, see-through blouses, and floor-length skirts sewn from pieces of this and that. Wearing velvet in the daytime. Wearing five strands of beads, never less. Wearing five, sometimes eight rings on my fingers. I'm so pleased that the fifties are popular again because the sixties can't be that far away. Just the other day I came out of a health-food store in Venice. A young couple came toward me. His hair was long and unruly, and he wore a jeans jacket, a pink shirt, and a scarf for a headband. She had let her punk haircut grow out, and she was wearing a long skirt of several fabrics, an Indian gauze blouse, a flowing shawl, several necklaces, bracelets, and other bangles. They made me so happy. I went running home shouting, "I told you, I told you . . . the sixties are coming back!"

—Rochelle Reed

The Seventies

Before the fashions of the seventies could emerge, the sixties had to run their course. Such an unconventional, peculiar time needed a few extra years to wind down. At the close of 1969, we weren't through with attention-seeking, figure-flaunting, and thumbing our nose at conventional ways.

The year 1970 was a year with no predominant look. Walk a block or so on any big city street, you'd see women wearing Indian block-print bedspread dresses, tight tie-dye T-shirts and hip-hugger jeans, afros, boots that hooked up the front, long calico dresses, rose-printed black-challis dirndl skirts, maxicoats, and microminis (slips that year came in twelve-inch lengths!).

The furor over the midi continued. Georges Pompidou and Richard Nixon went on the record as being for, and Paul Newman and the Lieutenant Governor of Georgia (the midi made strange bedfellows) against. The Lieutenant Governor announced, "If any girl ever comes in with one of those midi things on, I'll have her kicked out of the senate." The midi was called a fashion Edsel. Socialites organized POOFF (Preservation of Our Femininity and Finances) to quash the long look and urged women everywhere to sign a written pledge not to wear the midi. The audience applauded New York designer Mollie Parnis when she declared that "In this age of emphasis on sex and youth, no woman is going to add twenty years to her age by wearing skirts below her knees."

Knitted hats were Ali MacGraw's most imitated look. She pulled them down low in front to accent her dark eyes. We pulled ours down too, big eyes or not. We were fascinated by her style, creativity, and self-confidence, which were apparent in everything she wore from simple jeans to full-blown gypsy ensembles. (Griffin Productions)

Ali MacGraw was wearing her knit cloche hats, and we had to have one in every color, especially black. We didn't have Ali's eyes any more than we had Audrey's, but just like Ali, we'd pull the hat down to brow level and over the ears. It looked like a knitted helmet like that and made long hair a necessity. That hat could make any outfit look chic. We wore it with maxicoats and minidresses (which we wore together—a strange combination, flirtatious but warm in winter, until the wind blew), with gypsy dresses, and with long sweaters and jeans. For extra panache we threw a six-foot-long scarf around our necks and over our shoulders.

The early seventies had three outlandish fads: clunky platform shoes, long dresses in the daytime, and hot pants. They were more sixties than seventies in attitude. And once they were over, the freakiness was over.

The platform shoes started showing up in the late sixties. First, an inch or so was added to the sole, then two or three. A platform or a wedgie heel was one thing, a platform toe, another. It looked orthopedic. Why would anyone choose to wear platform shoes if they didn't have to? Some fashion commentators theorized that they were a way of balancing the sexy mini look. It cut the seduction aspect of the mini drastically to see a sweet young thing in these clunkers. The shoes eliminated the wiggle in the walk too. To our distorted sense of attractiveness, flats and regular pumps and sandals looked all wrong—incomplete. We liked the clodhopper look. The platform wasn't any more comfortable than the spike heel. It kept the foot rigid and made the wearer clomp along gracelessly, as if she were walking in skates. It didn't look too, too bad with pants, but it sure could drag down a good mini look. Even boots (by now shoe wardrobe essentials) were platforms.

Hot pants were the death rattle of the revealing sixties styles. The name alone was enough to sell them and to make men salivate. Really just old shorts done up in satin and velvet and marketed by Madison Avenue, they were the rage of 1971 (more fashionable in the winter when they were totally inappropriate than in the summer when they weren't). The fad was not born in the world of *haute couture,* although in a reversal of the old days, several couturiers, like St. Laurent, responded to the trend by including them in their collections. Hot pants were the creation of the trendy European boutique designers. The look jetted across the Atlantic on the butts of celebrities like Elsa Martinelli and Ursula Andress. Suddenly Alexander's in New York sold 1500 pairs in one week. A Seventh Avenue executive saw the writing on the wall when he told *Newsweek,* "We don't control the ladies. They control us now."

We thought hot pants looked good with boots, even better with bright tights and boots, which turned them from teen fad to sophisticated outfit. If we thought we could get away with it (and women were getting away with plenty by that point), we would wear them to restaurants, to the theater, and toned down with a blazer, to work. We expected Joan Kennedy to wear them . . . but Jackie did too. There were bridal hot pants in white satin, and hot pants with a sterno can appliqued on the rear pocket.

While they were actually more modest than the mini (no crotch shots now), they were perceived, even in their heyday, as more exotic than miniskirts. Nurses and grandmothers never wore them.

Hot pants were the shortest fashion fad this side of the ratty raccoon coat revival in 1957. They stayed in long enough for us to have our pictures taken in them. Somehow we knew we'd never believe it down the line if we didn't have a photograph.

The mod and hippie looks were often combined. Black tights, jean shorts, a blue workshirt, clunky clogs, and a bandanna tied low on the head was one get up. Or a skinny ribbed turtleneck topping hot pants, or jeans with a heavy leather belt slung low on the hips.

For women who couldn't stand the midi one year, we sure bought a lot of granny dresses the next. They evolved out of the hippie style with an overlay of Edwardian. We wore ankle-length dresses and skirts all day—calicos, ginghams, patchworks, denims, tartan plaids, velvets, lace-trimmed and tie-dyed. It wasn't modesty. It was merely the style. It was a quaint look and could be hippie or tailored, depending on the fabric. Long skirts seemed to express our back-to-nature, return-to-a-simpler-time, antiplastic yearnings. We needed some assurance that the world wasn't changing too fast. For comfort we turned to home-baked bread, macramé, and Laura Ashley dresses.

Long skirts had their logistical problems. They literally swept the floor. They got caught in escalators, elevator doors, drawers. For office wear they were as impractical in their way as minis were in theirs. But women wore them regardless. Visions of Guinevere and pre-Raphaelite splendor at the typewriter. It was, most of all, a romantic look, even when tailored. It certainly wasn't a realistic approach to dress. The high priestess of this style was an English de-

By the seventies we were drawing our fashion inspirations from everywhere and everybody, even from the hooker in the movie Klute. *Jane Fonda wears a braless midi look—a really confusing fashion (and sexual) statement. The skirt is split way up the front, but the boots look more witchy than wicked. P.S. We copied hooker hairdos too.* (Warner Brothers)

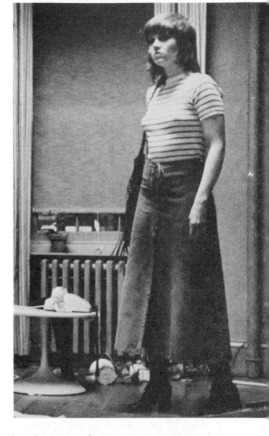

signer, Barbara Hulanicki. Her Biba designs—long jersey gowns, laces, and leather—were snapped up by London working girls. The style jumped the ocean and was picked up by American manufacturers like Gunne Sax and Arpeja who sold millions of Edwardian-Victorian dresses. Young women went wild over Arpeja's Young Edwardian line—dresses appliqued with floral motifs—and gimmicky tops from Organically Grown. Most of the romantic-Edwardian-Victorian clothes were contrived and overdetailed.

The St.-Tropez skirt, an ankle-length swirl of J-shaped gores done in alternating fabrics, was the look for the summer of '73. We still looked to the French Riviera for summertime inspiration. Not just for beach or barbecue, the skirt was worn for school and work. It was a non–dress-for-success year.

In the late hippie era we liked our T-shirts skintight and our jeans faded. We bought jeans used or prebleached. We cut the inseam open and made skirts. We appliqued them with rainbows. We studded them till they weighed almost as much as we did. We cut them in squares, mixed up the squares from several pairs, and sewed them together in a patchwork. Or striped patchwork. The fussier, the better. We wore patchwork jeans, jackets, and pantsuits to places that only a few years before would have required a dress, gloves, and a hat.

While clothes were fussy, make up and hair weren't. If there was a note of sanity in the typical hippie regalia, it was the fresh, natural face. The black eyes and white lips of the mini look were scrubbed away. Wigs were discarded. Long, straight hair and no makeup were the ideal.

The hippie look was many things: sloppy, creative, unstudied, studied, uniform, eccentric, and most of all, casual. That casualness is its legacy. Of course, true hippie garb went to the extreme of casualness, unkempt. But it drew our attention to just how uptight, plastic, cookie-cutter-correct we had been in our dress. Whether in Jackie Kennedy A-line outfits or Mary Quant minis, we dressed in packs. The only avenue open to us to impress other people was through correctness. The hippies spit on that idea. They felt clothes should be a form of expression and that people should be comfortable as well. These are lessons we are finally learning—but by fits and starts.

About 1973, the freakiness settled down and the real seventies style emerged. It can best be described as conservatism with a choice. Instead of one-look-at-a-time, a certain latitude was given that few of us found difficult to accept.

Skirt lengths varied between midcalf and midknee, with some variation each year. Some years seemed to feature fuller looks (wide skirts, gathered blouses) than others (the retro look), but nothing was wear-it-or-die.

Much of the sportswear in the stores was mix and match and

Conservative dress in the early seventies was often just plain boring—like this outfit. The pants, fitting snuggly over the hips and loose from midthigh down, are topped with a pleasant-at-best polyester print blouse. Accessories were trim: a narrow metal belt and low-heeled moccasins. (Columbia Pictures Company)

toned down from the sixties. For a while we out-drabbed each other in conservative browns and beiges and felt nervous in any display of plumage. We wore flannels, tweeds, plaids, and challis florals. Silk became affordable (not cheap but possible) and accessible to a generation brought up on synthetics. Silk was a novelty, but its timeless appeal was undeniable, and we scrimped to buy silk blouses in every color. We worried about how to clean them later. Silk was sexy but classy—and that's what we were after.

The dress-for-success school emerged as a result of women moving into more professional jobs in greater number. They needed suits and conservative dresses. Some felt they had to dupli-

Dress-for-success at its sexiest: Faye
Dunaway in Network. Her silk
blouse is open a little too far down for
real women to wear to work. But the
subtle colors, quality fabrics, and im-
peccable tailoring set an example for
the newly emerging career woman.
This is what investment dressing is all
about; this 1976 outfit could be worn
to a board meeting today. (United
Artists Corporation)

cate men's ensembles—a dark suit with a vest, a tailored shirt, and a
briefcase. The look was very hard-core, and was finally recognized
as more than necessary to be taken seriously. The clichéd but effective softening agent was a soft bow at the neck. Other women felt
that their goal was to dress on a par with men but not to imitate
them. Suits didn't have to measured by "Could a man wear this if it
had pants instead of a skirt?" Women could wear well-tailored suits
in burgundy or dark green and look quite professional, while men
would have looked dreadfully tacky in those colors. Dresses could
be foulard print silks with a coordinated blazer.

  With the new consciousness that women had to dress the part if they wanted to rise to the top of the corporate ladder, it was possible to stand on any downtown street corner in America during lunchtime and know the secretaries from the professionals. Secretaries dressed like girl friends, provocative and fluffy and fussy.

The dress-for-success look called for better clothes rather than more clothes. You could wear the same gray suit twice in one week, if you wore a different blouse each time.

Mary Tyler Moore's newsroom wardrobe was a forerunner of the dress-for-success look. Mary's work wardrobe (mostly by Norman Todd, a reasonably priced designer line that most women could find in stores) was neither housewife perky or secretary silly. It was sharp. It was somewhat serious. It was also short. On syndicated reruns, when Mary runs into Mr. Grant's office in a knee-skimming skirt, our reaction is "What is she thinking of?" At the time, it didn't look so awful. Besides, other than that, she looked great.

Following on the heels of the tailored pantsuits in the late sixties, evening pants took a new turn. Palazzo pants took all the fabric that minis left over. The widest had four yards in each leg. Palazzos looked free and easy, but they could be tricky. They really belonged at home. Otherwise heels would get caught in hemlines. Because they were pants, not skirts, they couldn't be pulled up when sitting down no matter how full they were.

Jumpsuits—not men's work cover-ups but something new—in fashionable colors and fabrics were more practical, until you hit the ladies' room. Then you understood why they were originally designed for men.

Tunics and pants were popular because we thought we were hiding big hips, big bosoms, thick waists, and saddlebags under the tunics. They were comfortable. They were an outfit that women who wouldn't put on pants could wear. We didn't even need a girdle. Hmmm. Done in the right fabric—a matte jersey or a polyester print knit—and worn with high heels, tunic-and-pants ensembles could be worn to dinner or parties.

In the seventies pants showed more variation within any one year than the whole of the fifties. Some were hip-huggers, some

The Mary Tyler Moore Show *was a clothes-watcher's delight. But Mary's look now seems too neat, too proper. Her wardrobe was relentlessly fitted. Not in a cheap or tacky way (after all, this is Mary Tyler Moore we're talking about) but very close to the body. Phyllis's and Rhoda's look was too trendy to hold up over the long run, especially the shoes. What we admired and copied most was Rhoda's headscarf, pulled down over the forehead and tied at the back of the neck.* (MTM Productions)

were waist-huggers. Some fit like a glove, others were pleated and baggy.

Suits were no longer only matching skirts and jackets. Non-suit suits were more creative: velvet blazers with plaid or challis floral skirts. Perhaps a matching challis shawl went *over* the blazer (or over a sweater and was tied at one hip—one fall, that style was all the rage).

Sportswear became more than mix-and-match Evan-Picone. It was down jackets and Frye boots and most of all, jogging outfits. The seventies turned into a time to wear jogging outfits when you weren't jogging, running shoes when you weren't running, tennis

When Carol Lynley was a teenage model, she could sell us everything from Clearasil to Jonathan Logan dresses. Here, in her movie star days, she dusted the floor in a bell-bottom outfit with a daring exposed midriff. (MGM)

outfits when you weren't playing tennis, and dancewear when you weren't dancing. Health and exercise became a way of life and by extension, a way of dressing. We wanted to show off the bodies we had worked so hard to acquire. Sweat-suit chic was (and still is) a practical, comfortable approach to fashion but again it was a uniform.

Caftans offered as much freedom as jogging suits but usually appealed to the more sedentary types. In cotton gauze, polyester print knit, or luxurious silk, caftans could be worn to poolside, to party, to dinner, but we finally grasped the idea that they weren't appropriate for work or school. They could be Halston sleek, ac-

cessorized with pearls and high-heeled sandals, or ethnic with amber
and silver necklaces piled on.

Sexiness in clothes became a function of slinky fabrics and
cleverly placed slits. Skirts slit up to *there* made slips inconceivable,
unless the slips were slit too. Some women thought that a hip-slit
gray flannel suit was a dress-for-success look but quickly retreated
from such folly—too much time spent fending off office passes and
clutching at the flap to look decorous in a seated position. Blouses
were slit down, down, down, left unbuttoned, maybe with no buttons at all. Peter Pan collars be damned. The come-on was no
longer the possibility of a crotch shot (once the slit-skirt fad passed)
but the possibility, even the likelihood, of seeing a breast or even a
nipple.

And what you couldn't see through the slits, you could see
through the fabric itself. Silks, jerseys, cotton knits were all worn
braless and girdleless. Minimum attire for being seen in public was
reduced to a dress and pantyhose. Why, that made strip poker a
two-round proposition.

Luxury lingerie was big business in the seventies. If not silk, we
had at least the appearance of silk, even in nylon tricots. Camisoles,
teddies, and step-ins, rich with lace, accounted for much of the display space in department store underwear sections (now renamed
"lingerie" or "intimate apparel"). Bras, panties, and slips were
mere wisps of silk and lace and so pretty they were a shame to hide.

And after all the new technology had created synthetics that
met our every need, we found one more necessity: natural fabrics.
Cotton panties were best, most hygienic, after all. Cotton bras with
demure lace were rather sexy.

Some women have given up bras for life. Others find them un-
necessary under bare summer clothes. But most women, having
flirted with the possibilities of wearing no or almost no underwear,
have decided that bra-wearing is for them. The girdle, however, is
dead, except for the most tradition-bound women who still think
that all that discomfort is an acceptable price to pay for thinking
they look thinner (in general, they don't). But what women aren't
spending on girdles, they're putting into camisoles and teddies and

slips. Those matching sets are irresistible . . . and expensive. Underwear, as long as it's sexy, is not dead.

Disco dressing skewered our fashion budget. We had to allow more money for dance clothes like spandex jeans, slinky silk crepe de Chine dresses, and the highest, skimpiest sandals. We could barely hobble across a crosswalk in some ankle-strapped creations, but somehow we managed to dance in them all night.

We began advertising our availability with T-shirt slogans proclaiming, "Hot Stuff" and "This Space for Rent." All sorts of double-entendres were emblazoned across our chests. We didn't have to reveal our actual body; we could be as provocative in print as in person. We told ourselves it was just for fun, and that we didn't really mean anything by it.

Mostly we took fashion seriously. For one thing, clothes were getting very expensive—no more $2.98 Ship 'n Shore blouses for us. Calvin Klein silk crepe de Chines were the state-of-the-art. Fashions in the late seventies (judging from what little perspective we have) were wonderfully good-looking. Good ideas, good colors, good fabrics. Styles were rich and varied (silks, cotton gauze, linen, wool jersey—and blends of those). But there were still some pixilated moments that are hard to comprehend. Like having to roll up the cuffs of jeans one spring because to wear them the right length was deemed *très outré*. Like white ankle socks on women, the same women who, twenty years before, knew with absolute certainty that only nerds wore such socks. Like having to roll up the sleeves on short-sleeved T-shirts. Like pushing up long sleeves to below the elbow (but never wearing them cut to that length). Like having to have buttons and tabs sewn into the sleeves to hold up cuffed, long-sleeved shirts in loose folds at the elbows (and wishing you could cut the damn things out—you couldn't—the next year when they rendered perfectly good silk shirts obsolete).

Although we had thrown away our long Indian block-print dresses (or used them to wash the car—with, not in), we found that India offered us a more mainstream fabric: cool cotton gauze. It took dyes well, so we were able to pick the most luscious colors—raspberry, blueberry, tangerine, lime—or just white, natural, or black. Gauze was recognized as the coolest of summer fabrics, and even when the fad had peaked, women couldn't give up such a practical fiber.

We pooh-poohed polyesters now, no longer dazzled by permanent press or clothes that dried in an hour. Bonded knits bit the dust. The time it took to iron a blouse or dress was worth it in terms of comfort while wearing it. Unbreathable polyester could feel like Saran Wrap on a hot day. To get us to spend our dollar, polyesters now had to imitate natural fabrics quite closely (silk, cotton, wool), or be blended with them for the best of both worlds.

On the brink of a whole new age of dressing as individuals, we crept backward. During the sixties we had been raising our clenched fists to Paris for telling us what to wear. Suddenly we could wear what we wanted, and what happened? We picked granny dresses and hot pants. Like kids who can choose their own food and order Twinkies, we were ordering junk. We needed if not parents, at least experts. So once again we turned to designers, the all-knowing guardians who would take up where our mothers left off—advising us, guiding us in matters of wardrobe.

They guided us into jeans. Jeans, glorious jeans, were the uniform of the late seventies, not faded, bleached, studded, patched, or painted, but dark, as God intended denim to be, and skintight. (One ad for "lean as a bean" Calvin Klein jeans boasted a sixteen-inch leg—which makes that sixteen-inch sheath of Dorian Leigh's all the more unfathomable.) We dry-cleaned our jeans, babying them like the most delicate silks. Cut was everything, and who knew better how to cut than designers. We would pay an extra $20 a pair to have Calvin or Pierre or Gloria stitched on our butts. We would swear that nobody made jeans like Calvin or Pierre or Gloria or whoever. We were designer conscious and designer specific.

Women in the seventies could wear anything, anywhere, but all they wanted to wear was jeans. With the riches of the world available to them, they dressed with the monotonous uniformity of medieval serfs.

A wardrobe of jeans could bog down the fashion industry. Fashion had to move on, and quickly, to keep the coffers flowing. But women weren't budging. They loved their jeans. So designers decided that jeans could stay indefinitely as long as minor changes were made each season so that women would have to buy a new pair. Tight cigarette legs one year, stovepipes the next, then cuffed, then baggy, then baggy with a tight cuff; we played musical jeans. If you wore a pair for too long, you were out of it. Cuffs in a non-cuff year were such a *gaffe* that you might as well have been wearing a Villager shirtwaist.

Still, it wasn't the old designer-as-dictator stuff from the fifties. First of all, designers were no longer remote Parisian couturiers who turned out just $1000 creations. In the seventies a designer was anyone who could get his or her recognized name on a label at the nape of the neck. And we recognized a lot of names: Willie, Stephen, Betsey, Calvin, Ralph, Gloria, Diane, Clovis, Oscar. Even Frenchmen like Cardin and Bohan were turning out moderately priced clothes. We had our favorites—Betsey for fun, Diane for her office-to-dinner wraps, Calvin for his simple but sexy silks. And . . . everyone for their jeans. The designers couldn't dictate very well because they couldn't seem to come to a consensus on anything except jeans.

Although we were sheep with jeans and jogging suits, we were able to explore some sense of individuality in other areas of fashion. We had to work through this new freedom slowly, always keeping a pair of jeans ready for when the choices were too overwhelming.

Harriet Selwyn's Fragments look was an example of the new creativity at its best: the jersey tent, surplice top, wrap skirt, and T-shirt came in all sorts of odd colors, and the point was to combine them in individual ways: back to front, two tops at a time, whatever. It was both clever and simple. Fragments came and went, but the attitude stayed with us.

The Annie Hall look brought a new gamin to our attention. Diane Keaton, like Audrey and Ali, had great personal style, but much more irreverent, even whimsical. Audrey was intellectual, Ali was artsy, but Diane was kooky. She wore men's clothes, grandma's clothes, and designer clothes, all at the same time. Baggy pants, men's shirts, pinstriped vests, floppy felt hats, longish skirts, clunky boots—a new antistyle, and much harder to achieve than it looked. Our mothers thought we just grabbed blindly in the closet. We

The classic Annie Hall Look, which was after all really the Diane Keaton look: men's vests, ties, baggy pants, big jackets, floppy hats, and Frye boots—all endearingly too large. Seemingly masculine, the look was really quite feminine because it made women seem fragile and tiny inside those oversized clothes. The look was an offshoot of the more mainstream mix-and-match layered look of the late seventies. (United Artists Corporation)

knew we had to play pattern against pattern, texture against texture if we were going to pull it off.

While the Annie Hall look itself was eccentric, the basic concepts were part of everyday office dress in the seventies: separates, different textures like cords and tweeds, vests. Layering. The middle-of-the-roaders just did it in clothes that fit.

By the end of the seventies, we were loosening up our jeans-as-entrée mentality. We saw the problem with uniform dressing. So what if jeans and a silk blouse could take us anywhere? Once we got there, we would find a dozen jeans-and-silk-blouse clones all around us. Perhaps we would try black jeans, or red or purple. Perhaps we would try something other than jeans.

* * *

Can we find happiness in the post mini, post hippie, post jeans era? Do we want real clothes after all? Do we need *in loco parentis* designers to tell us what to wear to work tomorrow? And in this age of designer-as-entrepreneur, of hundreds of thousands of women wearing the identical Liz Claiborne sweater, is individuality possible? Is creativity relegated to putting this year's Anne Klein jacket with last year's Ralph Lauren skirt and a blouse from Calvin Klein's collection a year before that?

Every department store in America carries the same lines. Evan-Picone, Calvin Klein, Gloria Vanderbilt, Liz Claiborne, St. Tropez West, Albert Nipon, Polo head the list. The colors are bright but limited. Twenty-five years ago we were limited to white, beige, red, black, and navy. Today our palette is black, white, turquoise, hot pink, and jade green. Heaven forbid you should want a Dartmouth-green skirt or a periwinkle sweater. Even if you found a periwinkle sweater, you'd never find anything to wear with it. Try to find old rose in a hot-pink year. We confuse brightness with choice. Today the sameness in our clothes is more a function of color than style or shape. Shape, finally, is limitless.

Leg-of-mutton sleeves, fine. Raglan sleeves, fine. Skintight sleeves, fine too. Miniculottes, great. Midcalf plaid full skirts, terrific. A three-inch-wide tight belt or a waistless shift, wow to both. A classic blazer or a square-shouldered waiter's jacket, yes yes. Preppie or punk. Spike heels or Capezio flats. Peasant blouse or silk shirt. The eighties *are* the fifties, the sixties, the seventies. Bought new, bought old. If only we'd saved our old cashmere sweaters, our black flats, our wide cinch belts. If only we had closets to store everything we ever bought and the foresight not to discard them the moment they began to look dated—to store it all on hangers, in the dark, waiting.

I was very influenced by Diana Rigg in the English TV series *The Avengers.* I wore jumpsuits and even made a few for myself. I owned a short reversible cape and, heaven knows, that wasn't a fad.

—Joan Borgman

The one fad item I vividly recall from the late sixties was my black wool, double-breasted maxicoat. I put it on layaway at a big department store (I'd never used layaway before), and my boyfriend surprised me and paid the balance on it and presented it to me as a gift. What a coat! I wore it with a red felt, big-brimmed hat and a nine-foot-long white knitted scarf to keep out the winter chill. This is one of the single best garments I have ever owned. I always felt terrific in it. How many peace marches did I go on in that coat? Every Christmas when I go back to Iowa to visit my family in that frigid country, I drag it to the cleaners (it must weigh fifteen pounds) and spruce it up for its yearly run. I know it's unbelievably out of fashion and looks it, but fashion be damned! I don't care how I look, it's still a great coat.

—Annette Swanberg

In 1970, I embraced the longuette-maxi look. I was in New York at the time. I remember attending the wedding of a friend in Maryland, wearing the new look and being told by my friends I had been in New York too long.

—Tristine Berry

I remember wearing a pantsuit to work for the first time. I'm a math professor at a technical college, so naturally we don't want to corrupt the youth of America (as if we could). I was convinced I would be called in by my president and fired on the spot. As I left the house in my brown-and-beige plaid pantsuit, my mother tried to hold me back, saying, "You can't wear *that* to work." I think it was 1966. "Why not?" I said. "Everyone is wearing them." Her comment was: "The students will be able to tell that your legs go all the way up." I tried to reassure her. "Mom, I think they already know."

I felt the same trepidation when I wore that first pair of white boots to work, not knowing how the president would react. (Don't forget, those were the days when male faculty members were fired for growing moustaches.) "Oh," he said, "I'm so glad you're wearing boots. At first, I thought you had two broken legs." I always did love those white boots and was saddened when they became passé, worn only by tacky little old ladies.

—Nancy Porter

WOOL COATS
come on strong
from hood
to hemline

1 Zip-front coat with attached hood . . and simply great in woven wool bonded to cotton. Note the button-tab closing at neck; welt seaming in front and back; in-seam pockets; 2 back vents. Acetate satin lining. Boots sold on opposite page.
Junior sizes 5, 7, 9, 11, 13.
Please state correct size.
V19 G 3179F—Bright red
V19 G 3180F—Tan
V19 G 3181F—Black
Shpg. wt. 5 lbs. 6 oz. . . . $39.90

2 Slate blue tweed coat . . a super example of what the longer length in coats is all about. Just-so styling includes a row of buttons down front and flap pockets with button trim. The warm-up hood buttons on and off. Wool bonded to cotton knit, acetate taffeta lining.
Junior sizes 5, 7, 9, 11, 13, 15.
Please state correct size.
Shipping weight 5 pounds 9 oz.
V19 G 3182F $47.90

ORDER YOUR USUAL SIZE
If in doubt, see page 749

JUNIOR BAZAAR

280 Sears

Women who rejected the midi accepted the maxicoat with welcome arms. It made midwinter mini-wearing much more tolerable. These coats stayed in style for several years and were just as appreciated over granny dresses. (Sears, Roebuck and Company)

This is the look of the Yves St. Laurent pantsuit that got women in pants in the late sixties—but hardly the fabric. This Sears version came in scroll-patterned double-knit polyester Perma-Pressed. (Sears, Roebuck and Company)

In 1970 or 1971, we were finally allowed to wear pantsuits to teach in. But it had to be a suit, not just pants and a top.

—*Linda Finch*

In the late sixties one woman in my office decided to singlehandedly break the pants barrier. No woman had ever worn pants to work. She started wearing trim, neat, conservative pants—perfectly respectable. She received a memo from the director regarding appropriate office attire. She responded with her own memo and kept on wearing pants. She stuck to it and finally "broke the system," and other women followed her lead.

—*Rose Mary Kimble*

We bought bell-bottomed jeans that were really tight in the thighs, then took them in another inch in the inside thigh seam the minute we got them home. Of course, they were almost impossible to get into, and you had to have a very tight belt to avoid disaster if you bent forward. They wouldn't pull up at all. It was vital that the bell part be as huge as the thigh was tight.

—*Caroline Winslow*

In 1973, you could wear absolutely anything (long skirts in the daytime, culottes, short skirts) and it was acceptable. Then we went back into a redefinition where you were judged a "professional" by the length of your skirt, and it seemed as though we were being put back into the same old cages of the past.

—*Nancie L. Porter*

I remember "falling" off those darned high platform shoes. Being only five foot one, I loved them because they made me so tall (plus I didn't have to have my capris shortened). When I liked something, I would go bananas and I'd buy it in all colors. So when things went out of style, I was in deep trouble. Like those five-inch-high wedgies. They came in seven colors, so I bought all seven colors. I was stuck with them. I still haven't learned my lesson.

—*Sherry Alberoni*

I bought two pairs of shoes in 1970 that I have saved all these years because they were so exotic. They were so extreme that I thought I

Mini and maxi were never meant to be worn together—but we did it anyway. Somehow we thought the maxicoat or vest was dynamite worn over miniskirts or hot pants. And just as subtle. A bare leg peeking out from between the flaps was meant to look as sexy as a bare leg peeking out from between the sheets. (Butterick Archives)

should give them to a museum. One pair had a solid-wood platform of five inches, covered with a printed floral fabric, edged in red-and-black suede with an ankle strap, and topped with a heavy metal studding of nailheads all over the place. They were the first of a trend to the very thick platforms, so I thought they were just grand. The print fabric on the base, a black-and-red small print, was a perfect coordinate to a long peasant dress I had just designed and made up. It was absolutely impossible to walk in these shoes (they weighed a ton) and it's a mystery to me why they were ever made. The other pair was made of clear Plexiglas and plastic. They were sandals on a Plexi base with clear, soft plastic-tubing ties that wrapped up the leg. The perfect shoe really, except they were once again uncomfortable but looked dynamite. Who cared about comfort when you could wear these modern Cinderella slippers with a minidress.

—*Barbara Diamond*

One of my favorite shoes of all time was wedgies—corkies, to be precise. I always wore the highest ones, a good four inches, and when I lived in Hollywood Hills and walked down to Musso and Frank's for dinner regularly, I always wore them despite the incline. I never thought a thing about it until a friend came from the East and marveled at my agility. I wish they'd come back into fashion.

—*Rochelle Reed*

I never wore a long skirt in public in the daytime—one of the few fads I had the brains to avoid.

—*M. Miller*

I know that two fashion trends—hot pants and long skirts—helped me both land and keep a job at the *Hollywood Reporter*. At age twenty-three or so, when I first started working there, a local promotion man came into the office with a pair of complimentary hot pants for me, bright yellow. I wore them with a workshirt (which I'd worn in Haight-Ashbury and had once been touched by Timothy Leary) and a broad, red-yellow-blue striped belt from France that actually belonged to my boyfriend. Of course, I wore pantyhose and high heels, and my hair touched nearly to my waist. I think I must have been quite a vision. I know that outfit won me a chance to cover a very big Writers' Conference in New York (my first trip) and no small number of lunches with famous men. Then long skirts came in and I bought a black one, which I wore with a plaid jacket and a large, floppy black hat and black boots. That outfit got me major interviews at the behest of the *Reporter* owners, who were pleased to have a reporter working for them who didn't come to work in shiny black pants like all the men. When I think back on all this, I'm as much embarrassed as amused.

—*Rochelle Reed*

I can remember every detail of a hot pants outfit I wore in 1972. It consisted of navy blue velvet hot pants, a white turtleneck, a long-sleeved sweater, a wide black leather belt at the hipline but higher

Women who wore minis to the office one year were wearing these long dresses the next—both impractical solutions to what to wear to work. Women who got in the habit of wearing the long length, never showing their legs, had a hard time reintroducing knee-length skirts to their work wardrobes without generating teasing remarks from co-workers. (Sears, Roebuck and Company)

Ex-Mouseketeer Sherry Alberoni called this "my good luck audition outfit" in the early seventies. "It got me Show Me America, *the Datsun girl, and* Victory Canteen." *What could be more American than a red, white, and blue hot-pants ensemble? Sherry added navy vinyl boots, with the popular but clunky heel of the time, and (of course!) pantyhose.* (Sherry Alberoni)

than the bottom of the sweater, and black leather boots. This was in Minnesota in March and it was still cold, so over this outfit I wore a Russian-style winter coat of black, gray, and white tweed with black fur at the collar, cuffs, and hem. The hem came to about midcalf. With the coat buttoned, I looked fairly ordinary, but when I opened it up I must have looked pretty strange. I felt really good wearing it because I knew I looked good. Again I was dressing with the idea of being noticed. It was more than looking good in the abstract or dressing the way *I* thought I looked good. Instead I was trying to look sexy or as close to it as possible. I'm not sure I'm getting across the distinction I'm trying to make. It was the difference between looking the way I thought looked good and looking the way I

thought someone else (usually a man) would think I looked good.
                                                                —*Sandy Calin*

Another of my favorite outfits was a pair of velour hot pants in royal
purple with boots (which I still have) to match, in purple suede. I
wore them with a white blouse, which was relatively tight-fitting and
open down to there! The gang went out to a club that featured good
beer, a bad band, and the opportunity to display one's hot pants in all
their glory.
                                                                —*Karen Berman*

Remember when we wore long dresses for daytime and dates? It was
then that I learned what was and what was not fashion. The minute
long dresses started going to the grocery stores, I knew they were
no longer chic and packed them up for posterity.
                                                                —*Barbara Diamond*

In the late sixties, early seventies, if it was old and used, it was perfect! Junk shops, Union War Surplus, and Salvation Army were
(and still are) my favorite shopping places. Hippie was in, and with it
came high-rise sailor pants, old musty lace blouses, and dresses my
grandmother might have worn. My favorite outfit of all time was a
long black dress I bought for seventy-five cents in a junk shop in San
Pedro. How I loved that dress. Long black flowing crepe, yard after
yard of it brushing the tops of my black patent leather platform
shoes. The top ended in an old-fashioned point at the waist. The
sleeves were long and full, gathered at the wrist with black velvet
ribbons. And to top the whole thing off, it had hundreds (it seemed)
of tiny covered buttons, fastened with loops, all the way down the
back. Just the thing for a Rolling Stones or Who concert.
    I still wear it today . . . only now I have to wait for October 31.
                                                                —*Pamela J. Baergen*

I have always loved the Greensleeves look (as I liked to call it) with
white peasant blouses, long peasant skirts, garlands in the hair. With
the advent of the hippie movement it was such a pleasure to be able
actually to find clothing like that to buy. I guess Gunne Sax is
the epitome of what I mean. And to this day, I enjoy this kind of
clothing.
                                                                —*Susan Stern*

When Ultrasuede first came out, I was crazy about it. Not only was it washable and hardly wrinkled at all, it was just like real suede. We all believed that. A miracle fabric. It felt so good and soft like real suede. So rich-looking. After all, Halston, such a big designer, was using it for dresses. Since I sewed, I was able to make a few skirts and even a shirtdress for much less than a Halston ready-to-wear. It was about $35 to $40 a yard then! Not cheap, then or now. But since it was so much like real suede that it was difficult to tell the difference (or so we thought), it was worth it. One day while I was shopping in a fabric store, a little five-year-old boy ran his hand down a bolt of Ultrasuede that was lying on a counter. He shouted, "Yuck! Plastic!"—my version of the Emperor's New Clothes.

—Ellen Ekman

Toward the mid-seventies, I discovered the women's movement and like any new convert, I went overboard. I stopped wearing makeup, stopped shaving my legs and underarms and stopped wearing a bra. I also started putting on weight, and my bust was never small. I do have a picture of myself without a bra (which I am *not* going to supply) and I looked awful! The strange thing is that I didn't feel all that good without a bra. I couldn't run because it hurt, and I was self-conscious about how I looked. But I was making a STATE-MENT, a political statement, and at that time, that was the primary concern for me.

Things have changed. After a period of dressing for men and the period of dressing for politics, I finally decided to dress for myself. I wear what is comfortable and what I think looks good. Now the criteria for looking good are my own, not somebody else's. I like tailored suits with pockets. I insist on pockets in all my skirts. When I'm pacing, I have to have pockets to put my hands in or I can't think.

—Sandy Calin

My mother hated the braless look, but she usually suffered in silence until I guess she couldn't stand it anymore. Then she'd say, "Will you please try to make an effort to wear a bra?"

—Manuela Cerruti

The bra slip appeared in the late sixties and was a godsend. If bought in nude, it would solve the slip show-through problem. If not

Diane Von Furstenberg (like Mary Quant before her) was always her own best model. Her sexy-but-sophisticated jersey wrap dresses were a uniform in the late seventies. They could be worn everywhere—to the office, to dinner, to brunch—and by anyone (the director of the company as well as her secretaries). (Diane Von Furstenberg)

available, one could buy a nude camisole to further preserve one's modesty against those who would see one's bra through light tops. Some fanatics on this (me) bought white camisoles and dyed them (poorly) in flesh. This tactic was, and is, motivated not so much by excessive modesty but by the desire for the style or pattern of one's top to be the focal point and not be disrupted by underwear lines.

—*Nancy Kinney*

The Nirvana of the clothes world would be achieved if only one had matching bras and panties at all times—you know, peach lace ensembles and white lace emsembles with little blue ribbons running through them. And of course a black set.

—*Nancy Kinney*

The look of the late seventies: casual, layered, and a mix of textures, fabrics, and colors. These fashions were finally comfortable. (Sears, Roebuck and Company)

If I were to say how my sense of fashion has changed over the years, I would say I now opt for comfort first. I will never buy high, high-heeled shoes again in my life. My years of wearing sandals and tennis shoes have made my feet too tender, and every venture into painful "real shoes" reinforces my decision. I still think they are beautiful, but not for me.

The other change is that even though I feel I now know what is fashionable or even trendy, and what would create a total look, I often choose to disregard pulling it all together. I choose this sometimes because of comfort, sometimes because of cost, and sometimes because of laziness. I don't want to change purses, find the perfect shoe, etc.

—Dawn Sturgill

In college I read in one of the fashion magazines that one should choose garments according to one's skin tone, not necessarily just to match hair or eye color. So I bought a nifty camel suit (wool gabardine, simple blazer jacket, and A-line skirt). It was a very classic style. I wore it constantly and always felt *well dressed* and good in it. This was one of the first times that I really paid attention to my skin tone in selecting color of a garment.

—Annette Swanberg

I passed the barrier of wearing pants to the office long ago and now mainly wear pants and jeans at home. I never wear jeans to the office. I feel they are not professional enough, although our office staff is extremely casual these days. If a worker wears a skirt or a suit, everyone immediately surmises she has to appear in court or has a hot lunch date.

—Dawn Sturgill

As I look back, I notice that most of the things I favored for comfort, ease of care, whatever, were not the things that men liked. Yet I suffered wearing a lot of things. Now I wonder, for whose sake?
—Sandy Whitehurst

Fashion Magazines in General and Mademoiselle's College Issue in Particular

We never would have known what to wear, or when to wear it, without the fashion magazines. They showed us what was best for the office, school, dates, or bed. They showed us how to look sexy, how to look demure, how long, how short, how much to bare, how much to cover.

Television couldn't fulfill our need for monthly fashion fixes. TV titillated our interest, gave us heroines to copy and first clues to a new look. But magazines taught us how to dress. Magazines were (and still are) fashion textbooks geared for both the beginner and the expert. We learned the finer points of accessorizing, hairdos, and makeup as well as about the clothes themselves. From the earliest teen years, when we turned to *Seventeen* (instead of our mothers) for advice, to well into middle age, when *Vogue* and *Harper's Bazaar* showed clothes that a mature woman could wear and afford, there was always a magazine to fit our needs. All we needed to bring to our monthly perusings was an interest in fashion. There was a great disparity in what we could actually buy. Some of us shopped at Lord and Taylor in New York, some of us shopped at Junior Miss in Florence, Alabama. But the magazines offered all of us the same inspiration.

Vogue and *Harper's Bazaar* were always the sibyls of high fashion, veritable mouthpieces for the couturiers. It was difficult to identify with much those magazines had to offer. We might have admired a Mainbocher suit in a remote way, but rarely did we think, "I've got to have it," as we did with the Evan-Picone and Arpeja clothes we saw in *Glamour* or *Seventeen*. *Vogue* and *Harper's Bazaar* were always monthly exercises on how the other half lived. It all seemed so stilted, so arch, and wasn't much more than a good giggle. The models of the fifties were either haughty sylphs like Dorian Leigh and Suzy Parker or waspy young society matrons who modeled for the magazines as a lark. Often these postdebs were real mothers (if not real people), and the copy prattled on about their doing without cooks but needing a full-time nanny. They'd be photographed at their country estates or city apartments. *Vogue* didn't have much to do with life in Levittown, but it was an amusing fantasy. We never really wanted to be the people on the pages of *Vogue,* but we liked looking in the window.

The *Vogue* and *Bazaar* clothes were for another life-style, another species, another galaxy. Not life as we knew it. In the fifties, *Vogue* did try to humanize its August 15 issue by dubbing it the "College Issue." The models were definitely not coeds (no Vassar '57 tacked after *their* names). The gauntest, most jaded New York models were decked out in plaids and jumpers. The fashion editors would add a bit about what to wear to the dean's tea (follow their advice and entering freshmen would look as mature as the dean's mother) before going on to cover the Paris balls. *Vogue* sponsored an annual contest; one coed, some well-connected postdeb at a Seven Sisters school, would receive the magazine's "coveted Prix de Paris." That was the sum of *Vogue*'s college issue. We were un-impressed. The college issue sham was dropped by the sixties as *Vogue* pursued its wild and wicked photo program: Veruschka, Tree, and Shrimpton in painted skins (both their own and those of endangered species) more than real clothes. August came, and *Vogue* opted for coverage of the new fall collections rather than for back to school with Betty Coed.

Glamour and *Mademoiselle*, however, knew how to put out a college issue. One we would begin anticipating around the Fourth of July, checking the newsstands regularly until the day it finally arrived. From the moment we ran home from the newsstand, we pored over them like reborn Christians studying the Bible. They were Baedekers for the Bobbie Brooks set, dog-eared from daily use and carefully hidden from nosy younger sisters with no respect.

More than twice as thick as any of the other issues during the year, they were a paean to the latest, most-sought-after, most ac-ceptable, most collegiate styles. Their appeal was far from limited to actual college girls. Mere high school freshmen could read and day-dream. More than being just a catalog of the latest fall fashions, the college issues presented us with a total package. By devouring every word, lingering over every picture, we could imagine being the best-dressed coeds ever—pert, well-coiffed, color-coordinated—all while managing to get straight As and despite a hectic social sched-ule. To look back over the college issues of *Glamour* and *Mademoi-selle* for the last thirty years is to see those times partly like they were and partly as we wished they had been.

Glamour featured ten college girls each August: cute, bouncy, popular coeds each of whose list of clubs and extracurricular activi-ties took up three inches in their yearbooks. They modeled the most wonderfully coordinated outfits, and the copy told us enough about each one so that we felt we knew her a little. They were sort of like Playmates but fully dressed.

Mademoiselle's college issue focused on a group of Guest Edi-tors who had won the magazine's yearly college competition. Win-ners were invited to New York for a month, in June, to guest-edit the August issue. The entire issue was a mix of real-life Horatia

Alger stories and fabulous clothes. A dream come true for this
year's girls gave the rest of us plenty to envy. Perhaps next year we
would enter and win, be feted all over New York with dancing,
dining, and going backstage at Broadway shows.

The *Mademoiselle* girls were artier, more creative, more driven
than their *Glamour* counterparts. They didn't necessarily turn up
modeling fall fashions (they didn't necessarily look like models). To
introduce each G.E. to us, they were photographed once or twice in
black and white, either in a group or yearbook style. But their
names appeared all over the issue—quoted, by-lined, they were
gossiped about like celebrities. We got another glimpse of them
(why, they felt almost like friends by now) when a photographer
went along to capture their interviews with real celebrities like
Ogden Nash, Truman Capote, and Stephen Sondheim.

What they wore on these interviews was their own clothes—
what they had packed for the trip to New York. Their outfits were
not as slick as the professionally coordinated, straight-from-the-
showroom ensembles on the other pages of the magazine. They
gave us a clearer picture of how what we wore changed over the
years.

Sylvia Plath is more noted for being a *Mademoiselle* G.E. than
are many of the other young women who went on to as much, if not
more, fame and fortune. In 1953, she set out to interview her celeb-
rity in a perfect city-summer dress: a sleeveless print shirtwaist with
a big white collar. In 1955, a sedate Gael Greene interviewed Gore
Vidal; she was in a prim outfit complete with hat and gloves and
Mamie Eisenhower bangs. That year another G.E., Joan Didion, in
a pageboy, looks surprisingly undated almost thirty years later,
because her hairstyle was longer and softer than the typical fifties
tight cut.

Ali MacGraw, going under the name of Alice MacGraw, was
not only a 1958 G.E., but cover girl for the college issue. Few
G.E.s were cover-girl material. Wearing a bright orange sweater
and gray skirt and leaning against a bicycle, Ali has a clean, clear
look that almost transcends the fifties. She remains one of *Mademoiselle*'s best-looking G.E.s ever. We should have known that she

was going places. She, too, wore a hat and gloves to her interview (with e. e. cummings), but at least the hat was a beret instead of some stiff chapeau.

The copy that G.E.s wrote was a bit more cutesy than their older colleagues turned out on a regular basis. Copy was kept college-oriented at every possible turn: "Coordinates Einstein never dreamed of." But we gobbled it up anyway. In an "open letter to a man with a crew cut" in 1953, the G.E.s reveled in the discovery that the new fashions were "just as good for girls and boys"—daring copies of Eton and Norfolk jackets, trench coats, and a liberal use of khaki. "We put a trouser cuff on a straight skirt" was meant to boast of their cleverness, but it's hard to picture a much sillier skirt than one with a cuff.

The G.E.s may have seemed hell-bent on a career in the fifties, but they were writing for a readership with more a modest goal—marriage (or at least engagement) before graduation. Yet the fashions for the college issues seemed much more career-oriented, serious, and tailored than they became in later years, when a much higher percentage of coeds were actually interested in a profession after graduation. The dress-for-successors of the late seventies had nothing on these fifties college girls. They might have been candidates for their MRS (as the old joke goes), but they dressed the part of rising young MBAs from Wharton. Throughout the editorial pages, tailored dresses and suits were shown on real coed models in campus settings. Now, this will come as a shock but here it is: They wore hats, gloves, and high heels on campus. Second shock: College men wore suits. Slacks and Bermuda shorts (nicely tailored in gray flannel or plaid) were strictly for leisure time, photographed in parks and bowling alleys (did we really bowl that much?).

Pages were devoted to date dressing: semi-casual dresses and suits for Friday nights (with gloves), black for Saturday night. Dating meant high heels and pearls. "Dressing for a quiet evening" in 1954 meant a two-piece Kimberley-type knit dress, heels, and gloves.

With a month in New York behind them, the G.E.s were quick

to advise us on the latest fall trends. We loved them for it, never thought we were being talked down to. In 1955, they let us in on the secret that charcoal green (what could that be?) was proving competition for gray flannel. And that man-made satin was giving tulle a run for its money in party clothes. The G.E.s also tipped us off to new color combinations like red and camel.

When a group portrait was taken, the G.E.s posed in identical outfits: twenty capes or Glen plaid suits or whatever was new for fall. In 1956, all the G.E.s posed together in look-alike fur-collared suits. Real college coeds (but not the G.E.s) posed for most of the fashion layouts. We always considered this an extra treat, the inspired touch being that each model was identified (Holly Hayseed, University of Iowa, 1958). But these twenty- and twenty-one-year-old girls looked so old, more like their own mothers. Too many neat hairdos, too many gloves, too many tailored suits. The models were always the same ages, year after year, but they began to look younger as styles loosened up.

Mademoiselle always deemed it necessary to devote half a dozen pages to formal dresses. In the early fifties we were smothered in vapid pastel tulle styles. Finally in 1958, formals (they would have us believe that no girl left for college without at least two formal gowns) took on a more sophisticated look: hot-pink satin, harem skirts, smooth lines instead of relentless ruffling.

By 1959, college clothes, like clothes in general, were starting to loosen up. Ali MacGraw, in a special encore (unusual for G.E.s) modeled a hot-pink sweater with a purple shirt. Literally shades of things to come. Saturday night dates were still black-dress territory. *Mademoiselle still* had its standards of appropriate dress. The spread on a fashionable weekend at Dartmouth showed a coed being welcomed at the station by an Ivy League contingent. She had on a neat little dress, gloves, and shoes with two-inch heels.

In 1959, the dressy layout featured jewel-tone satin gowns (accessorized with armpit-length gloves). Jade and emerald ballgowns, long and short. We flipped past those pages quickly.

In 1961, when the G.E.s were photographed en masse in hooded capes, they looked like alien beings. With the exception of those silly capes, college fashions seemed more and more relaxed: more separates, more plaids. G.E. makeovers included sleek hairdos with the new guiche curls.

In 1962, there must have been a big policy shift (or a much larger budget). G.E.s were treated to a trip abroad as well as the party month in New York. On the inaugural trip to Rome, they were herded up on the wing of an Alitalia jet to capture the event for *Mademoiselle*'s pages. They wore matching knit turtleneck dresses—perfect for Rome, we were led to believe (except perhaps in summer, which is when they went). Did this travel program signal a new world awareness? It seemed so. If for G.E.s, then surely for the rest of us too. Coed models were photographed in Paris and Segovia, not just on the library steps at NYU. G.E.s started looking like Jackie Kennedy that year. And they went to their interviews in Jackie-type dresses with ladylike pearls (but no gloves).

The next year, 1963, the winners went to Switzerland. Coeds were photographed in arty studio layouts. No halls of ivy, no streets of Montmartre. G.E. makeovers included lots of eye makeup and pale lips. Party dresses reflected Jackie too (slim, Empire designs).

In 1964, the most famous G.E. was Betsey Johnson. She fit right in with the new mod look, even as a college undergraduate. The college look, per se, was shelved for a while. G.E. interviewers wore sleeveless chemises with scarves tied at the neck. Only one showed up in a passé shirt-and-skirt outfit.

The mid-sixties college issues ignored the traditional college looks and opted for hip-huggers, minis with white lace pantyhose, and long hair. If you wanted the collegiate look, you were forced to search for Villager and Ladybug ads at the front of the issue. There you could still find floral shirtwaists—though mini-shirtwaists, to be sure. No black dresses for Saturday night dates. Date dressing now meant plaid taffeta minis with lace tights.

College girls were dressed like Beatle groupies. They wore the Carnaby look with flashy wide ties, skinny knit dresses, checkerboard knit suits. Coats, even to see University of Minnesota coeds through the winter, were above the knees. The models, generally long-haired blondes and Mary Quant-like brunettes, looked just plain dumb. They were still coeds, but they looked like go-go girls. Did these dimwits actually study anthropology or German lit?

The G.E.s' foreign flings continued, and in 1967, *Mademoiselle* introduced that year's winners in the strangest picture in the annals of their college issues. Twenty G.E.s posed at Machu Picchu, wearing matching plaid miniskirted suits and black tights. An accompanying article documenting their whirlwind trip to Peru was titled "We Conquistadoras." Were they helicoptered to the site, these modern *conquistadoras?* Or did the G.E.s, their chaperones, photographers, stylists, equipment, and suitcases filled with twenty plaid suits all make the harrowing railroad trip from Cuzco? What a strange sight they must have been.

There had been a slight subduing of the hard-edge mod look by then. It was evolving into a sort of Ivy League mod, which consisted of plaid minis, knee socks, sweaters, and slouchy hats. The magazine recommended vinyl thigh-high boots for campus, black minis for dates.

In 1968, Ann Beattie was one of the G.E.s in the group photographed at the ruins of Teotihuacán outside Mexico City. A perky paragraph always summed up each G.E. Ann, we were told, "collects hotel Do Not Disturb signs." The coed models looked not quite as dim-witted as in the previous years. G.E.s toured Mexico City (Ann Beattie modeled a mini-jumper as she leaned against the Aztec calendar stone), and back in New York, they wore their miniskirts to interview Peter Max and Dustin Hoffman.

In 1969, the mini style prevailed with micromini date dresses in pastels. The coeds looked like little girls. Hardly the look of serious prelaw or premed students.

A hint of hippie appeared that year. The political awareness of the times affected even the *Mademoiselle* staff. On the traditional page for the G.E. group photo on a plane wing or in some exotic ruins, *Mademoiselle* ran a dialogue in which G.E.s discussed the heavy topics of the day. (They got to go to Ireland that year, you'll be relieved to know.) "The midi is the message" for college, along with long sweaters, long scarves, knit hats, and boots that hooked up the front. Afros! Despite the midi edict, the G.E.s, a conservative group it seems, clung to their minis for their interviews with Kurt Vonnegut, Frank Stella, and William Kunstler.

The year 1971 was striking in its departure from the usual look of the college issue. Coed models suddenly appeared in jeans. Before then, *Mademoiselle* had never acknowledged that jeans existed, that they were practical in a college girl's wardrobe. Now there was an old-jeans-into-new-skirts feature, skinny sweaters, embroidered everything, patchwork coats. But our gals still wore minis to chat with Louise Nevelson, Pauline Kael, and John Simon.

Two men turned up in the group in 1972 and remained as token G.E.s in subsequent years. They always looked like they'd been sent to entertain the harem. The fashion pages were filled with jeans—faded, studded, embroidered. There was a sentimental visit to ex-G.E.s who had made it big like Ali and Betsey (who by that time was weird with a vengeance). And *still* the currently enthroned G.E.s wore minis to talk with Dick Cavett and Claes Oldenburg. Didn't the real *Mademoiselle* staffers pull them aside and clue them in about minis? Was there an *All About Eve* element to the month of June?

The next college issue visited not-so-famous ex-G.E.s, but it never struck us as a bit odd. Not everyone wore minis for the '73 interviews (with Bette Midler, Janet Flanner, and Joseph Papp). Some wore long skirts and bell bottoms. Not a pearl or a glove was in sight. The shoe feature was entitled "Gone is the super-platform, the exaggerated clunk. The real shoe is back," and then proceeded to show the 1973 platform look: inch-high platform toes. The orthopedic college look.

But in 1975, when the G.E.s proclaimed, "Blue denim forever" (good going, girls—only seven years after *Hair*), we couldn't see if they practiced what they preached. The interview photos showed only the subjects, not the interviewers. Were they in jeans, long skirts, Frye boots? Wasn't it our right to know? Perhaps it was better not to show them after all. Some of us were ten years past college by that point. Time to wean us of our college issue addiction. Maybe we wouldn't actually buy it anymore. Maybe we'd just browse through it at the newsstand.

ABOUT THE AUTHOR

Ellen Melinkoff, a free-lance writer in Los Angeles, is the author of *The Flavor of L.A.: A Guide to Ethnic Restaurants and Markets* (Chronicle Books, 1983).

She was born in Mineola, New York, in 1944, just in time to have had personal memories of the clothing in this book. She received her bachelor of arts degree in art history from the University of California at Los Angeles. She has been a social worker for Los Angeles County and an interior designer, and she now writes full time for such publications as *New West, Los Angeles Magazine, Los Angeles Times, Los Angeles Herald-Examiner, Travel & Leisure, The Washington Post,* and *San Francisco Chronicle.*